Basic Shiphandling for Masters, Mates and Pilots

P F Willerton, BSc., FNI
Senior Lecturer, Department of Marine Science
Plymouth Polytechnic

STANFORD MARITIME · LONDON

Stanford Maritime Limited
Member Company of the George Philip Group
12–14 Long Acre London WC2E 9LP
Editor D Nicolson

First Published 1980
© P F Willerton 1980
Typesetting by Malvern Typesetting Services
Printed in Great Britain by Ebenezer Baylis & Son Ltd
The Trinity Press, Worcester, and London

British Library Cataloguing in Publication Data
Willerton, P F
  Basic shiphandling for masters, mates
  and pilots.
  1. Shiphandling
  I. Title
623.88   VK543

ISBN 0-540-07333-4

Foreword

The safe and timely arrival of ships is primarily dependent upon the practical application of four basic seamens' skills: accurate navigation, safe collision avoidance, good seamanship and competent shiphandling.

Despite the fact that the art of shiphandling is fundamental to the movement of ships through the water, very few text books on the subject have been written and the reason possibly lies in the view, widely held among seafarers, that it can only be learnt from experience.

For some there is natural skill and instinctive flair while the majority learn from observation and instruction. In either case there is no doubt that experience and regular practice adds to the degree of confidence and ability with which they carry out their manoeuvres. To my mind, however, the modern seafarer needs to adopt a more professional approach and to understand the forces that influence his judgements.

With commercial pressures requiring the movement of larger and faster vessels and highly hazardous cargoes into more confined spaces, it is important that all ships' officers and pilots understand the basic principles of hydrodynamics and appreciate the effects of pressure distribution around the hull, in open and confined waters.

Sharing this basic knowledge provides a proper basis for communication, passage planning and an effective bridge team. I am very pleased to have the opportunity to write the foreword to this book which admirably introduces the subject of shiphandling in context.

Captain C. A. Rhodes, F.N.I.,
President, The Nautical Institute.

Preface

The art of handling water borne craft has been known to man from pre-historic times. Traditionally the skills required to become competent have been passed down from the master to his mates and apprentices. Little thought was given to the *causes* of a vessel's reactions to changing circumstances although a wealth of practical knowledge was acquired concerning the signs and symptoms of actual changes in situations, and the remedies available to counter such forces.

As steam power eclipsed the use of sail in commercial and naval vessels, some of this lore was, unfortunately, lost as the new systems gained reliability and credence. This process of change has continued and its rate increased. Ship sizes, shapes and means of propulsion have diversified almost immeasurably in recent years, and the cargoes carried and tasks required left several of Jules Verne's prophesies in their wake some years ago. An undesirable feature of this development, as recent tragedies have shown, is that the magnitude of the damage done by modern vessels has increased with the advance of technology.

These changes in ship design and use have been forced by the general replacement of labour by capital in almost all aspects of marine transport—a phenomenon which has required those personnel remaining 'aboard' to be educated and trained to a far higher standard than their predecessors. Whether or not this requirement has been fulfilled is an open question. Certainly recent enquiries by the British Government have suggested that a contributory factor in maritime disasters has been a lack of adequate training, and steps are being taken to improve the vocational training of British ship's officers. Similar policies are being followed by many of the more responsible nations of the world, however there remain ships sailing under flags which allow an owner's greed for short term gain to outweigh thoughts of tomorrow. It may well be that one of those 'albatrosses' is on a collision course with you! Due to the lack of education, training and discipline, fostered by a few, the reputation, status and advance of the seafaring profession runs the risk of being held back to the progress of the slowest and most unreliable.

In the 19th Century a seafarer might well spend his whole career working one type of ship in a very confined area of operations. The ship's officer of the last quarter of this century has had to be prepared to adapt himself to any part of the world in a matter of hours as he is flown to and from appointments. He must be ready to use a wide range of navigational and shiphandling systems with no time for any sort of practice, and fit into a team which may have met for the first time a few hours before in an airport lounge.

A public duty must exist to ensure that such officers are, firstly, educated to a high enough level to enable them to understand the changes about them and the reasons for those changes, and, secondly that they have full training in the operation of the particular types of equipment used in today's ships. The purpose of this text is to act as a 'bridge' between these two functions. The reader is therefore expected to have a basic knowledge of statics, dynamics, meteorology, oceanography, ship design, marine engineering and such other aspects of applied physics as are normally required of an officer or pilot under training. Having read the book, the author would hope that the student would enter a ship simulator, or, time, space and money allowing, an actual ship, to test whether or not the vessel's behaviour is as he anticipated, or if not why not.

In November 1977, the Nautical Institute held a conference on the subject of shiphandling. The purpose of that conference was two-fold, firstly to cover as many relevant topics as possible in the two days, with an emphasis on the need to pool the expertise of the Royal Navy, Merchant Navy and research organisations for the benefit of the serving mariner. Secondly to bring together basic information on shiphandling, as a subject in its own right, rather than as a part of the larger subjects of seamanship and navigation. It was the author's privilege to assist in the organisation of that conference and it was with pleasure that he received from the Institute the freedom to refer to the conference papers.

Particular thanks must go to the following, whose papers did much to inspire this book:

Mr. B. J. Ingram, Managing Director, Humber Tugs.
Dr. I. W. Dand, B.Sc, Ph.D, C.Eng, MRINA, Principal Scientific Officer, National Maritime Institute.
Mr. C. B. Barrass, M.Sc, C.Eng, MRINA, Principal Lecturer in Naval Architecture, Liverpool Polytechnic.
Mr. P. J. H. Tebay, F.N.I., Senior First Class Pilot, Liverpool.
Mr. R. S. Boyles, F.N.I., Pilot Manager, Manchester Ship Canal Co.
Dr. D. Clarke, B.Sc(Eng), DLC, Ph.D, C.Eng, MRINA, Principal Research Officer, British Ship Research Association.
Professor R. V. Thompson, B.Sc, M.Eng, Ph.D, C.Eng, F.I.Mar.E, F.I.Mech.E, F.S.E., Head of Dept of Marine Engineering, Newcastle University.

Basic Shiphandling for Masters, Mates and Pilots

Dr. J. W. English, B.Sc(WL Sch), Ph.D, C.Eng, FRINA, Principal Scientific Officer, National Maritime Institute.

Mr. A. A. Clarke, B.Sc(Tech), M.E.S., M.Inst.E.M., Head of E.M.I. Ergonomics Laboratory.

My thanks also go to Mr. D. C. S. Farquhar, Master Mariner, lately master of the S.T.V. *Tectona*, for reading the manuscript and offering technical advice. Lastly my thanks must go to my wife Anne without whom it can truly be said that this book would not have been possible.

P. F. Willerton

Plymouth, September 1979.

Contents

Chapter 1
The Ship and Her Environment

A vessel whether on the high seas or in a confined dock or harbour is continually being influenced by her environment. These influences can be from water movements, air streams or from pressures built up within these mediums. The sea is subject to movement in the form of tidal streams, ocean currents and waves generated by wind. These movements are familiar to us as changes on the sea surface but it must be borne in mind that the sea is three-dimensional, the surface water representing only one side of the figure. The air surrounding a ship must also be considered as more than a steady wind because it too is subject to variations of direction and velocity, and to vertical change.

Wind Effects

Leeway is defined as being the amount of drift of a vessel to leeward of the course steered, due to the action of the wind. It is, of course, related to the ratio of freeboard and top hamper on one hand and the amount of the vessel which is submerged on the other. Ships at their light draft, a dinghy with its centre board raised or a liferaft which has no drogue attached will all make a large amount of leeway compared with vessels in loaded condition or with a deep keel in the same wind condition. The amount of leeway made is usually treated as a quantity which has direction but no magnitude that is normally measured. It is expressed as the angle between the intended track or course line and the course made good, and named plus or minus (Fig. 1.1). Alternatively it could be described by a compass direction to leeward. For example if a vessel were sailing an Easterly course in a fresh breeze from the North causing her to be deflected 5° from the course line, then she is said to be making +5° leeway or 5° to the Southward.

In practice it is not usual to allow the vessel to make leeway as it is preferable to maintain progress along the charted course (Fig. 1.2). One exception to this is the case of a vessel sailing close hauled, as she cannot sail any higher without 'pinching' and loosing way. To stop the drift off course, a correction must be made to windward of the course to be

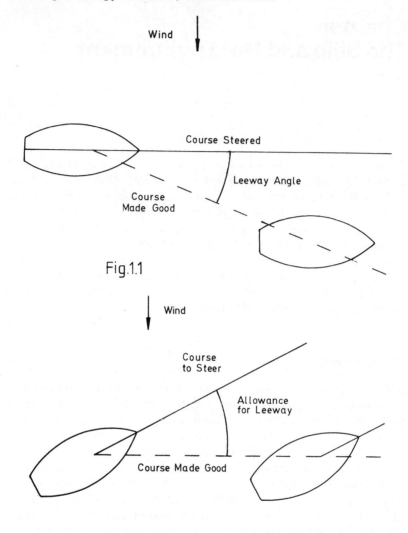

Fig.1.1

Fig.1.2

steered, the magnitude of this correction being approximately the same as the leeway made. To determine the amount it is best to fix the ship's position frequently and if there is a departure from the line on the chart ascertain its cause by:

1. checking the accuracy of the position;
2. checking that the helmsman has been and is steering the required course;

3. determining whether all or part of the offset is due to currents or tidal streams;

4. determining whether the prevailing wind direction and strength caused the effect measured.

If the reason is found to be leeway then the appropriate correction should be applied to the course steered.

Another method of assessing the amount of leeway is by looking aft and inspecting the angle between an imaginary extension of the ship's fore and aft line and the wake. If the wake appears to lead off to the windward side of the axis line then leeway is being made. This type of evaluation is difficult during darkness or in severe weather.

The condition of leeway so far has been in respect of a vessel underway in open water—a situation which any competent watch keeper should be able to take well within his stride. Other situations exist, however, where leeway is an important factor, for example in manoeuvring in enclosed waters and when stopped.

When a vessel is manoeuvring the wind can have an appreciable effect, and as the seaman must endeavour to use the wind and tide to his benefit, it is important that due allowance be made for windage when planning a manoeuvre in open water. Assuming that the wind is on the beam when a ship starts to reduce speed then the deflection from the intended track will increase in proportion to the distance steamed along that course. Eventually, if no other forces are acting, when the forward motion is off the ship she might be making considerable way downwind. It is unusual for a vessel to calibrate her leeway for differing values of speed, freeboard and windspeed. It is therefore, the seaman's task to use his knowledge and experience in anticipating the possible effects of wind as he reduces speed.

The capriciousness of the wind can further be observed when the vessel is moving in an enclosed dock or narrow waterway which has high buildings, hills or cliffs near by. In these cases it is quite probable that the force acting on the ship's hull will not be uniform in the fore and aft direction, causing a turning movement. Again the mariner must anticipate such circumstances by watching the sea surface ahead for patches of 'black water' which indicate areas of stronger wind. Other signs which are useful as wind indicators are smoke, flags and clouds. The presence of cumulonimbus clouds can give warning of squalls and violent wind shifts.

When a vessel is stopped in the water it is unlikely that she will drift directly down wind for a long period of time but more probable that she will suffer some degree of 'involuntary sailing'. This means that the ship's hull and superstructures will present an angle to the wind so as to cause some of the force due to the wind to be applied in the fore and aft line of the ship. The majority of the force will still be acting on the athwartships axis but the resultant will pay off on one reach or the other. This fact can, of course, have serious consequences when a ship is stopped and not under command off a coast which has the wind blowing parallel to it, because she will make a course towards or away from the coast and not parallel to it (Fig. 1.3).

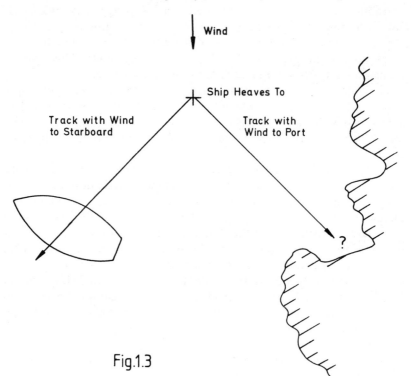

Fig.1.3

Thus the choice of which tack to heave-to on could be an important decision, for having once stopped, the mariner may be unable to alter his direction on drift. In some vessels it is possible to steer in this 'under bare poles' situation and turn from one reach to the other by gybing. A loaded all aft ship might in these circumstances make sternway, and therefore be virtually uncontrollable in such a situation. However, the great majority make headway. A colleague tells of sailing his tanker through the Sombrero Passage while engine repairs were being progressed. The best advice must be to take observation of drift patterns in changes of wind strength, conditions of loading and angle of trim.

The results of a mathematical simulation for a 270,000 d.w. tonne tanker indicated that although the aspect presented to the wind remained constant at about 60 degrees off the wind, both the rate of drift and the course made good altered significantly with draft. When she drew 9.14 metres the drift was at 3–5 knots almost down wind (3 degrees off), but when the draft was increased to 15.25 metres the drift slowed to only 1 knot in a direction 131 degrees off the wind; i.e. an alteration of nearly 50 degrees in the course made good. Thus the basic rules of heaving-to in a wind if a lee shore threatens are:

1. Put the vessel's stern towards the danger (if she tends to make headway).
2. If possible and time allows alter trim and draft to achieve optimum drift and course made good.

A further situation where the wind plays an important part is when a vessel is lying to an anchor or on an SBM (Single Buoy Mooring). One has only to watch a crowded mooring for small craft to see how vessels can be sheered about by the wind. Draft is again the controlling factor as can be quickly shown by comparing the behaviour of a light planing hulled motor boat with the behaviour of a deep keeled yacht. The light draft boat will sheer violently from side to side on the full scope of her cable.

A knowledge of these characteristics is important when designing an SBM for operation in an exposed position, in order that loading operations can continue with safety and speed in hostile conditions. The researchers can use computers to simulate these characteristics but the serving mariner is unlikely to have such sophisticated equipment to hand. He should bear in mind the likelihood of such behaviour when anchoring, both from the point of view of one's own ship and her arc of swing while straining at the cable, and also the possible gyrations of nearby craft which may be at radically different drafts and therefore adopt contradictory attitudes as the wind freshens.

Tide and Currents

The sea is never still for very long. Either the surface water is being disturbed by the wind setting up waves and drift currents, or tidal movement causes the ebb and flow of vast quantities of water. Whichever effect is present, (both can be) the ship is being borne along with the water mass.

Our knowledge of theoretical navigation teaches us to treat the tidal streams or currents as a vector and, knowing the ship's own vector, it is a simple mathematical task to determine either the effect of the streams (Fig. 1.4) or alternatively a course to counteract the stream (Fig. 1.5).

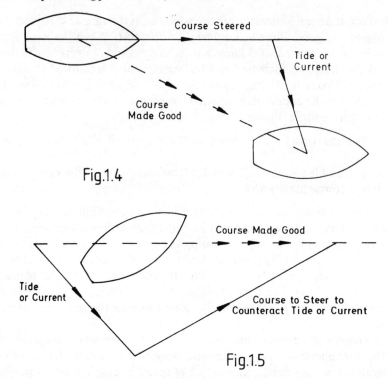

Fig.1.4

Fig.1.5

The source of information for the tidal data is from tidal diamonds or arrows on the navigational chart, from a tidal atlas or from such publications as the Pilot Book or Ocean Passages of the World. This information is based on averages taken over a period of time and thus in practice the mariner must consider whether or not the mean figures may have been affected by any meteorological phenomena.

Two examples of this happening are contrary winds and heavy rainfall. A wind of any strength will drag the surface water with it and if sufficient time allows over a great enough fetch then a current will develop. An approximate ratio of 40:1 between wind speed and current is the rule of thumb. With heavy rainfall on land and the rivers in spate, the tidal predictions for height, set and rate can be awry. A third example is that of a storm surge piling water against a coastline which will cause considerable deviation from the predictions. Therefore, those responsible for handling vessels where tidal streams or currents might be expected should look to the published information for guidance only. If allowance is to be made by adding some increment to the charted course then the effect of this action must be tested by checking the ship's position and if the ship is not in her estimated position, eliminate the other alternatives and take action to counter the actual force which is deflecting the ship.

The sea is of course a three-dimensional entity and although the competent navigator will watch for the direction and rate of the tidal streams by observing any buoys or piers he passes, these only give an indication of the surface movement of water. Vertical sections through the water show that due to density differences and frictional drag, the sub-surface water can be moving in the opposite direction at a considerable rate. A vessel of any appreciable draft will therefore be moved by the resultant of the tidal forces and not the force apparent on the surface. This effect is found in the deep oceans and in river and coastal waters. In the Pacific the Equatorial Undercurrent, or Cromwell Current, flows eastwards under the west going surface water of the Equatorial Current. Similarly in many rivers and harbours the surface water may indicate that the ebb has started and yet the level continues to rise, partially due to the sub-surface stream still being on the flood. When such streams are channelled around obstructions on the bed and banks of the river then very complex cross currents and eddies are formed, acting on the hull at different levels and varying distances forward and abaft of the ship's turning centre.

The Regime

The forces acting on a ship due to the environment must also include those due to the interaction between the hull and the surrounding water or the sea bed and river banks. These effects, most noticeable in shallow water, greatly influence the ship's performance with particular reference to the stopping and turning characteristics. Interacting forces occur in calm water as well as in a disturbed sea although in the latter case they are combined with the forces arising from wind and waves. Their effect on a ship can be such as to cause a rapid and violent change of course which may, if not controlled in sufficient time, lead to a collision or grounding.

When a ship is floating at rest in calm water the pressures acting on its hull are hydrostatic only. When it moves through the water hydrodynamic forces come into play which can be seen at the sea surface in the characteristic wave pattern which accompanies a ship in motion. The forces which act against the forward motion of a ship moving at constant speed, are due to these 'wave' pressures acting on the hull and also to friction acting over the wetted surface area. The frictional drag is kept to a minimum by maintaining the hull in a smooth and weed free state. The difference in performance before and after drydocking or slipping is usually noticeable and even without excessive marine growth can be as much as 10 per cent.

These 'wave' pressures can act in a differing manner and in open seas, clear of other ships, will probably be found to be positive near the bow, negative (outwards) amidships and positive at the stern though smaller than at the bow. This arrangement will result in an apparent sinkage thus increasing the draft (Fig. 1.6).

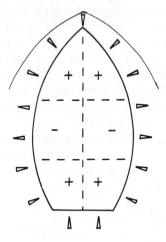

▭ = Direction of Pressure Force
+ or − = Sum of Pressure over Section
of the Hull

Fig.1.6

The downward displacement of a vessel moving through the water is known as *squat*. Squat is related to the vessel's speed, block coefficient and blockage factor, the blockage factor being the relationship between the ship's maximum underwater cross-sectional area and the cross-sectional area of the waterway through which she is passing. In open water the effective boundaries of the water which the ship is moving through are limited to the volume disturbed by the ship. This volume is of quite modest dimensions. However, when the bottom of the waterway is closed then the effect becomes more pronounced.

Consider a tanker 200 metres long making 12 knots through sea which is 40 metres deep. Her trim is 2 metres (down) by the stern. The squat will be about 0.3 metres aft and 0.4 metres forward. If the water depth is now decreased to 15 metres then the squat becomes about 0.9 metres aft and 1.1 metres forward.

Squat, in both shallow water and canals, can affect shiphandling by reducing the underkeel clearance available at any particular time. In general squat is 'by the head' for conventional displacement ships but as a ship is usually trimmed by the stern then it is rare for squat to cause the trim to become 'by the head'.

To add to the problem of an apparently increased draft due to shallow water, there is the additional hazard of interaction between the ship and the bottom or side of a channel, due to pressure changes occurring between the hull and these boundaries. This phenomenon is best understood if one first considers the flow of water past a ship's hull in open water. So long as the hull shape is symmetrical and the vessel is not heeled then the forces acting will be as described above and equal on either side. When a bank is present on one side this will cause an imbalance in the forces as pressure increases forward and decreases aft on the shoreward side (Fig. 1.7). Such a change in the delicate balance of pressure forces acting on a hull can cause large longitudinal and lateral forces coupled with powerful turning moments to be applied to the ship.

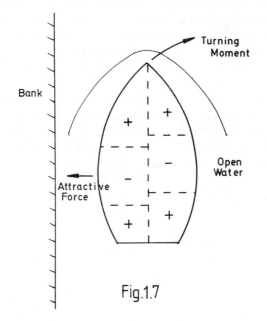

Fig.1.7

These may give rise to severe problems in handling the ship. A slight undulation in the seabed can cause a ship to change direction if the water is shallow enough—a phenomenon described by seamen as 'smelling the bottom'.

A third aspect of the nature of the surroundings of a ship's manoeuvring characteristics is resistance. This force is also particularly pronounced in a river or canal where speed over the ground will decrease as the blockage factor increases at the same shaft revolutions. There is in fact a 'limiting speed' above which a conventional displacement ship is unlikely to be able to proceed. It is therefore of little purpose to increase shaft revolutions in shallow or restricted water to try to make the ship go faster if she is moving close to her limiting speed.

The key to controlling the ship in these interaction situations is by carefully regulating her speed. This has the effect firstly of reducing squat and secondly of reducing resistance. When the blockage factor is approaching 60 per cent the speed has to be reduced to 2 or 3 knots. The opposite side of the coin is that to counter those forces, which are likely to cause longitudinal turning moments in the vessel, requires use of the rudder—also that the effectiveness of the rudder is greatly increased by the action of the race from the propeller. Therefore, to maintain control in interaction situations it would appear to be important to ensure that there is an adequate flow of water over the rudder blade, especially in shallow water. This can be done effectively if the rudder lies in the screw race by maintaining adequate screw revolutions. In certain situations it may be prudent to increase revolutions to maintain or regain control. A 'kick' on the engines to make the rudder bite, but not sufficient to cause the ship to gather way, is a useful aid for the shiphandler to remember.

In the preceding paragraphs some of the forces acting on a ship have been described, particularly those due to the wind and water movements and pressure on the ship's hull from external sources. These forces will be examined in more detail in the following chapters when specific shiphandling situations are considered.

Chapter 2
Ship Generated Forces

The form of a ship's hull, the response of its propelling machinery and the effect of propeller and rudder action will give a ship its manoeuvring identity.

The Hull

Merchant ship design is naturally influenced to a great degree by the commercial and economic considerations of the trade in which she is going to earn a living. The handling characteristics are therefore not primary factors in the architect's brief, these characteristics being fixed by the geometric size and shape, although some improvement may be made by cosmetic surgery around the stern and by altering the rudder shape. The addition of thrusters may also improve low speed manoeuvring. Of basic concern to the shiphandler is the question 'if I put the rudder amidships will the ship stop turning and follow a straight course?' The alternative is to apply opposite helm to control the swing. A ship which steadies without correction is said to be *dynamically stable*.

Dynamic stability is related to the following hull parameters: length, beam, draft and block coefficient. If a ship's length is increased her dynamic stability is increased, whereas increase in beam and block coefficient will bring about characteristic yawing past her heading. Deepening the draft improves dynamic stability and trim by the stern improves it further.

A ship with poor dynamic stability can effect some improvement by enlarging the rudder to a maximum of about 2 per cent of lateral underwater area. The result of being unstable in this context is that the helmsman will have to work much harder than in a stable vessel and as pilots, masters, officers and crew all have to take these characteristics as they find them, again it illustrates the importance of getting the 'feel' of a ship before reaching a close quarters situation. Nothing can cause more alarm on the bridge than when the helmsman, having complied with the order 'Rudder Amidships', gets no apparent slowing of the ship's rate of turn. The probable fault lies with the design of the vessel, her draft and trim, and not with the unfortunate man on the wheel. Supertankers tend to be dynamically unstable while ships with finer lines are more easily handled.

Distinct from the ship's response to her own shape and answer to the helm, is the magnitude of the turning performance. Ships plying in international trade require to have basic performance data on hand for a boarding pilot. This information includes a turning circle diagram at full and half speed, to port and starboard showing the time and distance of advance and transfer required to alter the course 90 degrees with maximum rudder angle and power settings. The advance and transfer are the distance the ship moves forward and laterally before the heading changes by 90 degrees (Fig. 2.1). The variables in design features again include rudder area and block coefficient, the former improving performance as it is increased to its effective limit, while for ships of the same length, beam and rudder angle the one with the greater block coefficient will have the tighter turning circle. Increasing the trim by the stern will make the turning circle larger, a trim increase of 1 per cent causing the turning diameter to go up by 10 per cent.

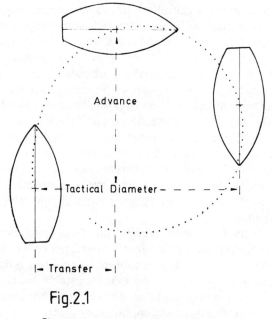

Fig.2.1

The turning characteristics of a ship

The ability to stop a vessel under control is also important and the time and distance taken to come to rest in the water, while maintaining approximately the initial heading and with minimum use of the rudder, should be recorded on trials and posted on the bridge with the other handling data.

An important factor when considering stopping distances is that the mass of a ship increases with the cube of her linear dimensions, whereas the braking effect of reversed propulsion and hull resistance increase with the square of those dimensions. This means that large ships travel a greater number of ships' lengths than smaller ones before stopping. It has been calculated that the force required to stop a VLCC within half its unassisted stopping distance would put a large rocket into Earth orbit. This is clearly impractical and the shiphandler must bear in mind the fact that larger ships have longer stopping distances and it is therefore necessary to reduce speed in ample time.

The situation thus far has concerned the hull characteristics of merchant ships, which tend to the 'box shape' to maximise cargo carrying capacity. Warship design, however, calls for finer lines and higher power-to-weight ratios. As a general rule such vessels have two propellers and twin rudders. This combination of engine power and application enables a modern destroyer class to stop in the water from 28 knots in 5 cables. Their ability to accelerate and turn is equally impressive and in keeping with their occupational requirement of being able to avoid incoming torpedoes and missiles while being able to fly off her own aircraft and hunt submarines. This makes their response lively and restraint must be exercised when handling such ships in confined circumstances.

Propulsion Systems

We have seen above that a ship's manoeuvring identity is directly related to her hull form, but its ability to obtain the best out of that hull form is a function of the power and action of the engines through the propeller and rudder system employed. The various types of engine available today have differing properties of size, weight, fuel consumption, response to control orders, starting time and stopping as well as their ease of repair and maintenance.

Motor Ships. The compression ignition engine is very widely used as it tends to be the least expensive to run. The usual means employed to start these engines is by injecting compressed air into the cylinders. This air is stored in a reservoir which is kept topped up by a compressor on the main engine itself. Thus if there are too many engine movements or mis-starts the reservoir will become drained as more air is being consumed than the compressor makes. Use of starting air is of lesser importance when a controllable pitch propeller is fitted because the engine is kept running in a constant direction. Similarly, when medium or high speed diesel engines are installed they are run constantly and a clutch used to transmit power to the shafts.

Low speed diesel engines operate directly onto the shaft and their full speed is of the order 110–150 rpm. Their response is second only to steam reciprocating engines which are rarely found nowadays. In addition to the limited number of starts in a short period of time, the shiphandler must also remember that difficulties can be experienced in starting the engine when still making a lot of headway. This is because the propeller will be trying to turn in the water stream and because of the direct drive the engine will be turning over in the ahead direction unless checked by a brake. It is best therefore, to reduce speed through the water before ordering an astern movement. It is quite usual to use light fuel oil rather than the more expensive diesel oil in low speed engines. This fuel oil requires heating before it can be injected into the cylinders.

Medium and high speed diesels are a popular arrangement in smaller vessels where one or more engines drive a shaft through a gear box and clutch. These types lend themselves readily to direct control from the bridge and give good service so long as they are treated with care. For example, the engine speed allowed to fall to idling revolutions before engaging the opposite gear. Many engines are fitted with a device to prevent the operator over-stressing the machinery in this way.

Other than this slight delay, such engines are very responsive and, like their low-speed relatives, can develop almost as much power astern as ahead; but, of course, the application of this astern power is less efficient as ship's hulls, propellers and rudders are usually designed to work in the ahead direction for most of their working lives.

Turbines. Although the steam reciprocating engine is a rarity, the steam turbine is found in large vessels and where sustained high speed is required, as in a container ship. The steam turbine is less heavy than its diesel equivalent and is more reliable. Its rate of fuel consumption is generally higher though and in this age of spiralling oil prices it is more expensive to operate for that reason, despite the determined efforts of the turbine builders to construct more efficient plants.

A turbine ship, while being smooth running and more reliable in the mechanical sense has one major drawback from the shiphandling point of view, namely that its response to control orders for changes of pace and direction of shaft rotation, are slow. Because of this slowness to develop power it must be given time to increase revolutions, and when stopped it must be allowed to run down. For astern power a separate turbine is employed which has perhaps only two thirds (in some vessels even less than this) of the power of the ahead turbine. Thus when manoeuvring a turbine driven ship each movement must be carefully planned as response to engine orders is not so rapid as with a motor ship.

In recent years a great deal of development has been done in the marine use of gas turbines. Few commercial vessels have them but naval craft are fitted with these engines. They are particularly suitable for the high manoeuvrability characteristics required of modern warships, being capable of starting from cold in a matter of minutes and having a very rapid response to control orders thus providing a major operational advantage of very rapid acceleration and deceleration. For astern power either reversing gear boxes or controllable pitch propellers are used giving ample astern power very rapidly.

Nuclear power is extensively used in large warships and submarines as a heat source for boilers feeding steam turbines. Some such merchant ships have been built but these have been commercially unsuccessful and because of hostile public pressure in some countries, their movements have been severely restricted. When accepted into port, they tend to be handled with great care because of the real and imaginary risks of radiation leaks—especially after a collision or stranding.

Propellers and Rudders

The ship's hull form determines the basic handling characteristics, and the choice of engine will add to this pattern by determining the power and response available to move the vessel. The third part of the operational aspect of forces inherent in the ship herself, is the manoeuvring unit or the propeller/rudder combination.

The propeller is usually fitted to the stern, this being the most efficient and practical position. As the ship moves forward some water flows aft to create what is termed *the wake*. The propeller operates in the flow and accelerates the water aft in propelling the vessel. A propeller works more efficiently in this wake flow, which is the reason for preferring single screw to twin screw ships; with single screws a greater proportion of the wake flows through the propeller (Fig. 2.2).

Because of the variable inflow the blades of a propeller operating in such a wake experience large cyclic fluctuations of loading during a revolution, the thrust on the blade at top dead centre being about twice the value acting on the other blades of a three bladed propeller. These fluctuating loadings are one cause of vibration found at the stern of ships.

The popular concept of propeller action is that of pushing the vessel forward because of high pressures induced on the downstream faces of the blades (Fig. 2.3). In fact, almost two-thirds of the thrust force arises

Fig.2.2

Wake streamlines through the propeller arc and over the rudder

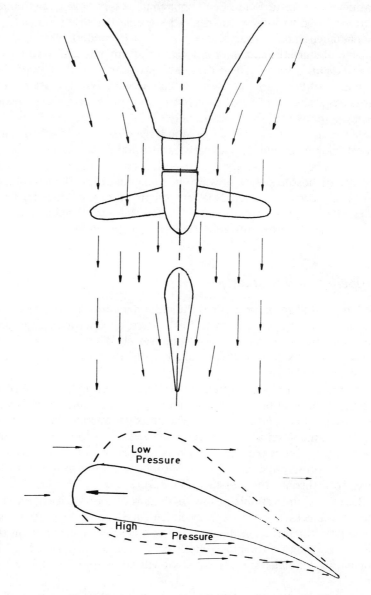

Fig.2.3

Pressure distribution over a chord of a propeller

from low pressure acting on the backs or upstream faces of the blades. This process is similar to the lift given by aeroplane wings and yacht sails. In the top dead centre position where the hydrostatic pressure is lowest and the thrust is high the pressures at the blade tips might well be low enough to reach the vapour pressure of water. If this 'boiling' does occur it is known as *cavitation* and makes a noise like gravel and stones being agitated in an empty concrete mixer; their effect is to cause erosion of the blades' surfaces and they are a further source of vibration at the stern.

Cavitation increases as irregular wake flow increases. Thus as the sea state worsens the flow will be disturbed, a factor which is made worse if the vessel is light and the propeller blades at or near the water line when at the top of their cycle. The rudder, which usually lies in the propeller slipstream, can be damaged by this cavitation and vibration. The longitudinal clearance between the screw and the rudder is critical in minimising this type of damage.

Propellers can be designed to turn in either direction when producing an ahead thrust. If they turn clockwise when viewed from aft, they are said to be *right-handed*; if anti-clockwise, they are said to be *left-handed*. In twin screw ships the starboard propeller is normally right-handed and the port propeller left-handed (Fig. 2.4). The reason for this arrangement of outward turning propellers is two-fold, firstly to reduce cavitation and secondly to take the greatest benefit from the paddle wheel effect or *transverse thrust* as it is more correctly known.

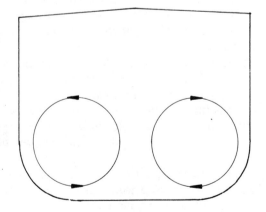

Fig.2.4

The conventional direction of propeller rotation
in twin screw ships

Transverse thrust is a phenomenon which is particularly noticeable when starting from rest until there is a wake flow through the propeller. This is because the forces generated by the propeller have a large athwartship component. The result of this is a wheeling effect in the direction of rotation. A right-handed propeller when going ahead will swing the stern to starboard and the bow to port. The bow will swing to starboard and the stern to port when the engine is reversed. Because the wake flow moves best over the hull shape when the ship is going ahead, the bias reduces as the ship increases speed and of course the rudder becomes effective. When going astern there is little wake strength at the propeller and it may not be possible to correct the bias and steer astern. This is a very important factor when planning a manoeuvre and as will be seen later it is preferable, if the option is available, to berth port side to, using the bias of transverse thrust to cant the stern into the quay.

The relationship between the rudder and the propeller is a very important one, because the efficiency of each is much effected by the position of the other. In a single screw ship with the rudder hung aft of the propeller a turning moment can be induced by the propeller slipstream acting on the rudder without the necessity of a wake flow over the rudder. Thus a 'kick' ahead on the engine with the rudder turned to one side or the other will result in the ship being turned without making much headway.

The alternative effect should also be noted that when the screw is stopped while making way it will be found that the efficiency of the rudder is reduced. When used in conjunction with the transverse thrust, that is in a turn to starboard with a right-handed propeller, then the resulting turning moment is greater than if the manoeuvre has been to port. The effect of either action is of course subject to the ship's dynamic stability which was discussed earlier in this chapter.

In a twin screw ship with a single rudder, the rudder does not have any effect unless there is either a wake flow past it or at low speeds the rudder is turned far enough to lie in the slipstream from one or other of the propellers. This means that a twin screw ship moving slowly or stopped is less sensitive to the helm than a single screw vessel. But if the twin screw ship uses her propellers in opposite directions then the turning circle is much reduced.

In most ships the maximum possible rudder angle is 35 degrees either side. This is an arbitrary angle which gives almost the full range of manoeuvring capabilities from the rudder without overstressing the rudder stock. There is some case for angles up to 70 degrees each side being available at zero speed. However, the service maximum angle at full speed is often voluntarily held to 15 degrees to minimise heeling and strain on the steering gear. If the rudder is put over 'too far' for the speed at which the ship is moving through the water, it will stall and lose its turning properties (Fig. 2.5). This stall occurs in the same manner as the air flow over a wing form or sail when an eddy forms on the unexposed side and becomes so large that it causes the flow streams passing the foil to collapse, reducing lift and causing loss of efficiency.

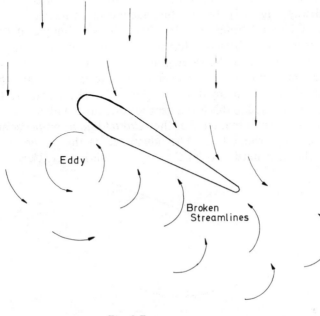

Fig.2.5

A stalled rudder

The propeller and rudder combinations discussed so far have been in use for the better part of a hundred years, generally keeping pace with the development in ship size and speed. However, in the 1960's and 70's economic pressures have resulted in re-examination by shipowners of their propulsion systems to make savings on fuel costs and harbour bills.

If, for the same power unit, greater effective thrust can be obtained by improving the design of the manoeuvring unit, then this is going to improve the service efficiency of the ship. An example is the ducted propeller which is particularly suited to ships with high propeller loadings. Tugs, dredgers, trawlers and more recently VLCC's often work in these conditions with high thrust, low speed and/or low swept area through draft limitations. The fitting of a controllable pitch propeller can also offer savings because the engine is not stopped during manoeuvring thus significantly reducing the wear and tear if auxilliary devices are fitted to assist manoeuvring, such as low thrusters or active rudders. Again, savings can be made by allowing the vessel to dock without the aid of tugs, because of her improved handling capability.

Ducted Propellers. With fixed types of duct, sometimes referred to as the 'Kort nozzle' or a shrouded propeller, the tail shaft is fitted in the conventional way (Fig. 2.6). In tugs this has meant an increase in bollard pull from 1.2 to 1.5 tonnes per 100 BHP. This technique of fitting a propeller in a duct has been developed further by using a right angle drive in which the lower or underwater gearbox bears the propeller and propeller shaft and can be rotated over a full circle; this means that the thrust can be pointed in any direction (Fig. 2.7). The nozzle around the propeller is connected to this lower gearbox and turns with it.

This latter system is marketed as the *Schottel Rudderpropeller* and it is fitted in many harbour tugs. The advantage of this rudder-propeller system is that it is harder to 'girt' a tug, or pull it over, because of its

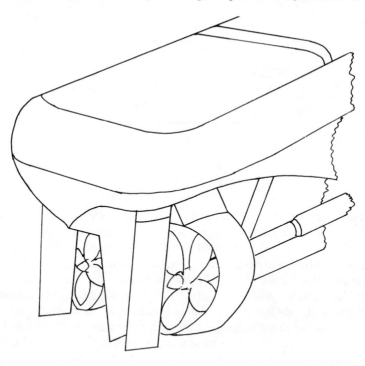

Fig.2.6

The after section of a tug showing shrouded propellers

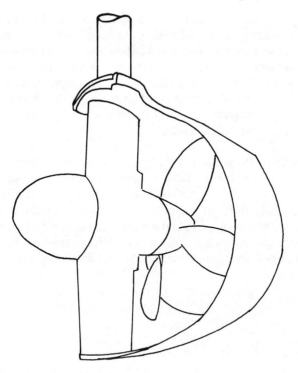

Fig.2.7

Right angled drive and steerable propeller

capability of applying sufficient thrust in the right direction to get out of trouble, which is not available to the conventional tug.

Controllable Pitch Propellers. CP Propellers are now fitted on many types of ship, particularly those with low speed manoeuvring requirements, where the speed of reversal of thrust or pitch change is beneficial and in ships with more than one loading condition, such as trawlers. The blades of the propeller are actuated by hydraulic fluid fed to the boss through a hollow drive shaft. In order to house the pitch change mechanism, the boss diameter is usually around 30 per cent to 35 per cent of the screw diameter. This larger boss involves only a small efficiency loss (1 per cent–2 per cent), compared with fixed pitch propellers, however the CPP permits the engine to be run at constant speed with varying ship speed, or with large variations in propeller loading such as occur when towing or running freely.

From the shiphandler's point of view the advantages mentioned above

29

must be offset against greater loss in directional stability when slowing down, particularly in an emergency, than with a fixed blade propeller and the bias when going astern is nowhere near as predictable. There is also the problem of mechanical failures which can result in something of a lottery as to which position the blades will adopt, neutral pitch, full ahead or full astern. The direction of rotation is often left-handed which means that the transverse thrust when the pitch is reversed cants the stern to port in the conventional manner.

Voith Schnieder Propulsion. This type of propulsion system is one of the few which do not use a screw to give the thrust. The shaft extends through the bottom of the hull to rotate a wheel to which are attached a number (usually four) of paddle shaped blades at right angles to the wheel and extending down into the water. The attitude of these blades is controlled from the bridge to direct the thrust as required thus enabling the vessel to be highly manoeuvrable. Small harbour tugs are often fitted with this system.

Thrusters

The manoeuvring systems discussed so far have been primarily concentrated at the after end of the vessel and have been arranged, whether as a composite unit or in combination, to propel steer the ship from the stern; although some turning moment can be induced by transverse thrust or use of propeller and rudder together.

These arrangements leave the bow of the vessel very much at the mercy of the external forces mentioned in Chapter 1. In recent years many ships such as coasters, rig supply craft and parcel tankers, which manoeuvre frequently, have been fitted with thrusters at the fore end to give positive lateral thrust to that extremity. These thrusters are usually mounted in a tunnel, athwart the fore peak tank. Ideally the tunnels should have belled mouths to improve the efficiency, but a compromise is often made with the ship's hull resistance, (which is not improved by such an opening); the leading edge is left square and the downstream edge recessed to avoid a drag increase. It must be realised that these devices are only efficient when the ship speed is zero. When longitudinal motion exceeds three knots the thrust from the tunnel is swept aft in the ship's stream lines and is wasted (Fig. 2.8). On the inlet side low pressure will build up and severe cavitation will occur.

The most usual form of thruster propulsion is by a CP propeller driven by an AC electric motor. This arrangement gives rapid response and reversal of thrust. The general criticism of thrusters, by shiphandlers, is

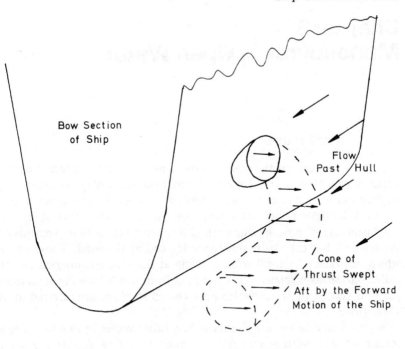

Bow Section
of Ship

Flow
Past Hull

Cone of
Thrust Swept
Aft by the Forward
Motion of the Ship

Fig.2.8

Flow from bow thruster

that they tend to be under-powered, but it must be remembered that the peak loading should not be so great that the ship's electrical system breaks down.

In some ships where operational performance is more important than mechanical efficiency, ducted propellers can be lowered beneath the hull to provide thrust in any direction and are termed *azimuthing thrusters*. These thrusters will be at a greater depth than the tunnel variety and therefore less affected by the sea state—cavitation is also a smaller problem. They are found in ships where station keeping at low or gear speed is required as, for example, with drilling ships.

Thrusters are occasionally fitted at the stern of ships but development of devices which utilise the power of the main engine to provide lateral forces (rather than fitting additional motors) is a more attractive investment.

Chapter 3
Manoeuvres in Open Water

Sea and Swell Waves

The surface waters of the world's oceans are constantly affected by the winds which blow over them and the part the wind plays in generating surface currents has been mentioned in Chapter 1. The other major effect is the development of waves. Not all the waves found at sea are wind generated; some are due to tidal flows and others to movements of the sea bed, but the vast majority are formed by the wind. Those waves which are raised by local wind blowing at the time of observation are called *sea waves* whereas waves resulting from winds blowing at another place or caused by winds which have ceased to blow, are referred to as *swell waves*.

Waves found at sea are similar to any other waves in that they are a means of transmitting energy, and must therefore follow the same mathematical rules. However, because these waves are often made up of many simple waveforms superimposed on each other, it is difficult to describe an 'individual' and easier to refer to the average. Waves in the sea are usually described in terms of speed, length, period and height (Fig. 3.1). The *speed* is the rate of progress at which a wave travels, expressed in knots; the *length*, in metres, is the distance between successive crests or troughs; the *height* is the vertical distance measured in metres between the top of a crest and the bottom of a trough; and the *period* of a wave train is the time between successive crests or successive troughs passing a given point. The relationship between these characteristics is complex in sea waves, but the speeds can be expressed as:

Speed $= 3.1 \times$ period knots
and length $= k \times (\text{period})^2$ metres
where k is variable between 0.78 and 1.04.

The height of a sea wave is not related to the above factors but to the amount of energy absorbed by that wave. It is found in practice that once the height to length ratio exceeds 1/13 then the wind will cause the crests to break. If the wind suddenly drops then a very steep waveform can exist for a little while.

It is not unusual for waves of dissimilar length, speed, height and period to be travelling in different directions. The result of this, parti-

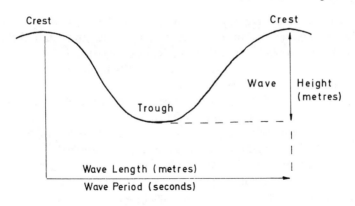

Crest

Crest

Trough

Wave

Height (metres)

Wave Length (metres)

Wave Period (seconds)

Fig.3.1

Characteristics of waves

cularly if the directions are almost coincident, is that a confused sea may occur with occasional waves in each system synchronising to give a wave whose height is the sum of the amplitudes of its component waves. The waves either side of such a large wave will decrease in height until such time as the trough in one system synchronises with the crest of a wave in the other, resulting in the trough cancelling the crest out and an area of relatively dead water will be found. This effect of waves combining is known as *grouping* (Fig. 3.2). The speed of advance of wave groups is found to be half the speed of advance of the individual waves.

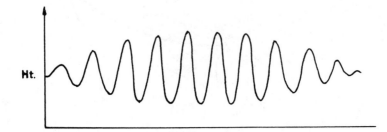

Ht.

Fig.3.2

Grouping of waves

Swell waves can travel many thousands of miles from their origin before dying away. They usually have a large wave length in proportion to height. The onset of a swell, particularly in tropical or subtropical regions, is perhaps the first sign of an approaching storm as the speed of movement of these waves is faster than the disturbance causing them.

When a wave enters an area whose depth is less than half the wave length, it undergoes profound modification. Its speed is reduced, its direction of motion may be changed and finally its height increases with decrease in depth until the wave breaks.

A knowledge of the formation and behaviour of waves is important to the seafarer as the forces contained in these systems will undoubtedly affect his vessel however large or small. These effects are of two sorts; those largely due to swell waves which alter the angle of the sea surface causing the ship to move in response, and the effects of sea waves which, because of the higher amounts of energy contained in them due to their greater height, will possibly cause damage as well as movement.

The movement of a ship in a seaway can be described in terms of the movement about the athwartships, longitudinal and vertical axis (Fig. 3.3). The characteristics of this movement are related to the hull form and the ship's stability. Her stability involves the relative positions of the centres of gravity and buoyancy, and her ability to remain right way up in different conditions of loading and sea state.

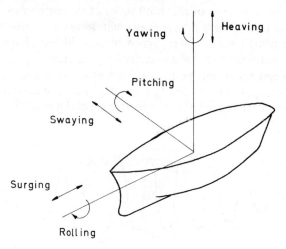

Fig.3.3

Describing a ship's movement
in a seaway

In general terms a vessel which has a full shape towards the ends will resist pitching, whilst increasing the beam will counter rolling. A ship which tends to top heaviness, without being unstable, is described as being *tender* and will have a slow, sometimes ponderous, rolling action. Alternatively when there is excessive weight in the bottom of the craft the movement is often uncomfortably rapid and the ship is *stiff*.

As was mentioned in Chapter 1 the wind associated with the build up of a sea can cause problems of its own, but once such a sea or swell exists then it too will affect the efficiency and handling qualities of the vessel not least in her ability to keep a good course. The force of breaking sea waves can be considerable, knocking the ship off her heading. If a swell exists the effect is for the ship to want to move down the slope, and again there is likely to be a deviation from the intended track. Difficulty is also experienced in maintaining direction and speed when the movement of the ship is such as to cause the streamlines flowing into the propeller and rudder system to breakdown. Indeed, at light draft the propeller may well be out of the water and thus totally inefficient.

Steering a Course Manually

Heavy weather procedures will be considered later but even quite moderate conditions can test a helmsman's skill. There are two basic effects to be countered in addition to any effects due to the propeller; they are, firstly, the general tendency of the vessel to adopt her natural angle to the wind and sea, and secondly, the pushing of the ship from her heading by individual waves. The helmsman must often keep a permanent bias on the rudder to counter the former, and steer positively to maintain course to overcome the forces of the latter.

The secret is to judge the amount of yaw and only allow rudder to counter the difference between the forces due alternately to wave ridges and troughs. It is wasteful of the helmsman's energy and causes excessive wear on steering gear to constantly try to maintain heading when the next wave will bring the vessel to very nearly her original direction. In these days of automatic steering it is useful to give crew members practice in taking the wheel when the vessel is in a seaway as a precaution against the day when the autopilot is not available.

Steering into a head sea requires a different technique to that employed when it is astern, particularly in a smaller craft. If the seas are of significant size it is prudent not to drive the ship into the waves but to try to ride them. If this method is possible it enables the ship to maintain more forward momentum as less energy will be absorbed by the oncoming wave. When the sea is astern then the problem is one of allowing the vessel to yaw but not to broach. The tendency for the stern to be lifted by the following wave if it is overtaking is natural and in relatively moderate conditions any sideways lift will be countered as the stern sinks back into the next trough, thus the ship will yaw about her course. In heavier weather the sea might push the stern well off line and also cause rolling leading to the vessel being knocked down or broaching. Great skill is needed to differentiate between the natural yaw which requires little correction and the occasional large wave that requires quick positive action. This has to be done solely from the helmsman's feel of the ship's motion as he can rarely see the waves approaching from aft.

One authority recommends that the good helmsman is an 'alert but idle man' for the less he turns the wheel the better course he will make.

Automatic Steering

Nearly all ocean-going vessels are equipped with automatic pilots which offer a saving in manpower, and under good conditions (when properly adjusted) are found more efficient than many crewmen if the magnitude and number of helm movements are measured. The fewer movements, the less drag is caused by the rudder, allowing the efficiency of the propulsive unit to increase. It is usual for most ocean-going vessels to steer by automatic pilot almost continuously while on passage and when traffic conditions make it safe to do so.

It must always be borne in mind that these usually reliable machines do suffer mechanical and electrical failures themselves, or are inoperable if the gyro compass fails. If the controls on the automatic pilot are not properly adjusted, an excessive number of rudder movements might be caused. These controls usually determine the angle of yaw that can occur naturally before corrective action is taken and the maximum amount of rudder angle which the machine can use. The settings will vary with the dynamic stability of the ship and the prevailing sea and weather conditions. The manufacturer's instructions should be consulted for more precise advice as to the best settings to be employed.

Turning Circles and Stopping Distances

Handling performance was discussed earlier as were the requirements for basic data on those characteristics to be posted on the bridge for the benefit of ship's officers and pilots. When considering the turning circle it must be remembered that the whole vessel does not follow the same path, but that the turn will centre about the pivot point which lies about one third of the vessel's length from the stem (Fig. 3.4). The stern will swing wide on the turn, not crossing the initial path until the ship has moved at least two lengths forward and then following a wider turning

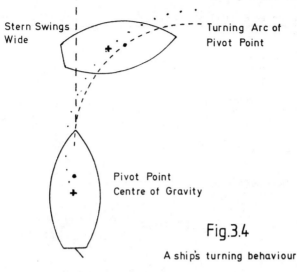

Turning Arc of C of G

Stern Swings
Wide

Turning Arc of
Pivot Point

Pivot Point
Centre of Gravity

Fig.3.4

A ship's turning behaviour

circle than the bow. The speed is likewise greatly affected by such a turn
because of the rudder drag and breakdown of streamlines into the propeller thus reducing its efficiency. After turning through ninety degrees
the loss will be about one third, reducing to about half the original
velocity when the course has been altered by one hundred and eighty
degrees. The above factors can be varied, as mentioned in the previous chapter, by altering draft, trim or loading and additionally the
turn, in one direction, can benefit from the transverse thrust of the
propeller.

Stopping a ship in an emergency depends firstly on the mass and its
velocity and secondly on the engine power available to bring the vessel to
a stop in the water with the minimum of deviation from the original
course line. A well tried method of using the engine to brake the forward
progress, is to initially keep the propeller going ahead but reducing the
revolutions and turning the helm from one side to the other to create
rudder drag. When the way has been reduced the propeller can be
reversed and astern revolutions built up as the speed through the water
declines, stopping engines when all way is off. Typical emergency (crash)
stopping distances and turning circles are shown in Fig. 3.5.

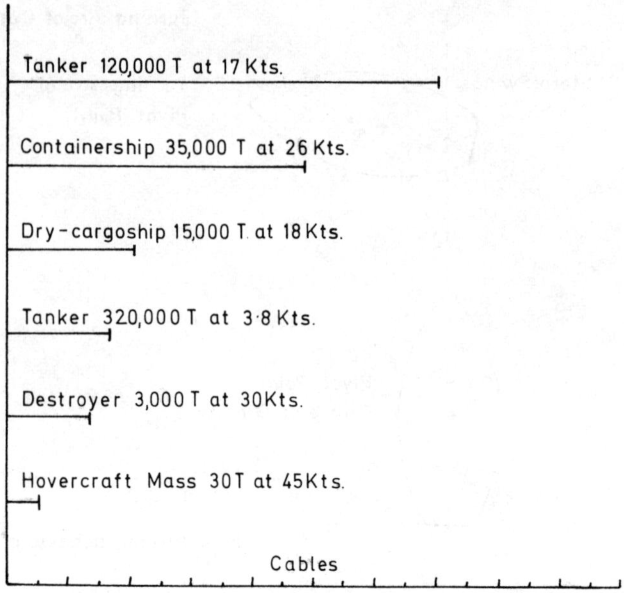

Tanker 120,000 T at 17 Kts.

Containership 35,000 T at 26 Kts.

Dry-cargoship 15,000 T at 18 Kts.

Tanker 320,000 T at 3·8 Kts.

Destroyer 3,000 T at 30 Kts.

Hovercraft Mass 30 T at 45 Kts.

Cables

Fig.35

Approximate emergency stopping distances

Collision Avoidance and Defensive Navigation

The duties under the International Regulations for Preventing Collisions at Sea frequently require that a watchkeeping officer shall manoeuvre his vessel to keep out of the way of another vessel, either when he is required to, to prevent collision etc., or because it is desirable to prevent a situation which might necessitate action under the rules. The latter system of conning the ship would seem to have come into greater use in recent years, probably with the advent of larger ships, more dangerous cargoes and an awareness that the other vessel may not abide by the statutory obligations which are about to rest upon him. The present case law on collision cases tells us that the Regulations do not apply just because two vessels are in sight of each other but only at a time when risk of collision exists. The ship's officer therefore has two choices, firstly to try to prevent risk of collision occurring or secondly, if it does occur, to follow the directions contained in the Regulations.

The first of the above options is an aspect of 'defensive navigation', and its execution depends upon several factors, including:

1. the manoeuvring characteristics of your own vessel;
2. knowledge of the presence, occupation and possible intentions of all other vessels within tactical range;
3. the sea room available.

It is plain therefore that an appreciation of the performance of one's own ship and the capabilities of all other craft found at sea should be within the ken of even the most junior officer in charge of a watch; not least the handling characteristics in existing conditions and depth of water. The 1972 collision regulations are now far clearer than their predecessors in respect to the speed a ship should be making and how that speed can be determined.

When the operation of large ships in open sea conditions is considered then it is probable that the tactical range is in the order of twelve to fifteen miles and risk of collision exists at six miles if the geometric parameters are correct. In restricted waters or heavy traffic these ranges will not apply because the safe speed will become lower and the efficiency of the watch increased by calling extra personnel to the bridge, changing to manual steering and putting engines on standby. Those in charge of smaller vessels must always bear in mind the magnitude of the stopping distances and turning circles of larger vessels when considering their own response to a developing situation. When risk of collision exists it does so between both vessels and should impact occur it is invariably the smaller which suffers greater damage if not total loss.

Occasionally, for some reason, a point is reached where collision becomes inevitable. However regrettable in these circumstances, the person in charge of the bridge still has a duty to the other vessel, his own crew, shipowners and insurers, to minimise the force of the collision and hopefully avoid a disaster. Meeting end on means that the subsequent damage will be proportional to the force due to both vessels' forward motion, whereas a glancing blow, when both ships are moving in almost the same direction at similar speeds, is far less likely to be the cause of serious damage. If collision is inevitable, the helm should be turned to steer the ship in such a manner that as much of the momentum as possible is moving in the same direction as the other vessel. If damage is to be sustained it is better to take it forward of the collision bulkhead or on the quarters, and avoid being holed in cargo spaces and accommodation areas when at all possible.

Emergency Procedures

Man Overboard. Should it be reported to the bridge that a man has fallen

39

overboard in the preceding few minutes then the first priorities must be to release the bridge wing life-buoy and its associated light and smoke floats and post lookouts to watch this mark. The possibility of avoiding a man by using the helm and engines, at this stage, are almost nil. A ship 600 feet long making 15 knots will cover her own length approximately every 24 seconds. Thus if engines were on immediate standby and the wheel manned, it is unlikely that there would have been much reaction by the time he passed the stern even if sighted going overboard right forward.

In conditions of reasonable visibility and sea state the quickest way of returning to a life-buoy is to put the wheel over to the side of tightest turning circle and con the ship back to the mark, turning onto a reciprocal course, by the time that point is reached (Fig. 3.6). The engines will now be on standby and arrangements in hand to recover the person in the water when he is sighted. This recovery can be made by launching a boat, or lowering a net or rope ladder. If necessary a life-raft can be used to give protection until a full rescue can be made.

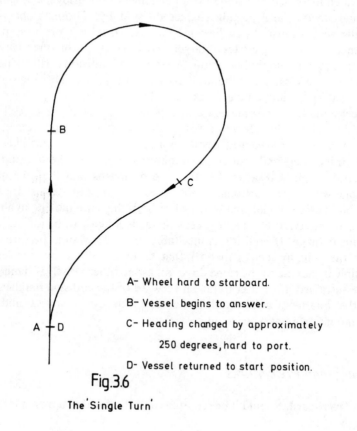

A- Wheel hard to starboard.

B- Vessel begins to answer.

C- Heading changed by approximately

250 degrees, hard to port.

D- Vessel returned to start position.

Fig. 3.6

The 'Single Turn'

In darkness, poor visibility or heavy weather, when it is unlikely that the light and smoke float will remain in sight during the manoeuvring, then the *Williamson turn* should be used (Fig. 3.7). This strategy has the benefit of bringing the ship back onto the reciprocal of her course line. It is performed by holding the wheel hard over in one direction until the heading alters by about sixty degrees. At this juncture the wheel is put hard over in the opposite direction until the heading is approaching the reciprocal of the original course at which time she is steadied and the search can begin as nearly as possible retracing the wake. An alert look-out is kept until the person is recovered or until such time as it is considered that further backtracking will be unnecessary as determined from the time at which the victim was last sighted. The ship should then be turned to search a line parallel to and to leeward of the original course line. Like other manoeuvres the Williamson turn should be practised to determine the initial angle to swing off course to port and to starboard, before reversing the wheel.

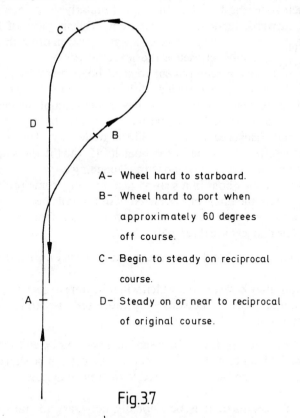

A – Wheel hard to starboard.

B – Wheel hard to port when approximately 60 degrees off course.

C – Begin to steady on reciprocal course.

D – Steady on or near to reciprocal of original course.

Fig.3.7

The 'Williamson Turn'

Launching and Recovery of Boats. When sending boats away at sea great care has to be taken to complete launching without injury to the crew or damage to the boat. The ship herself will act as a breakwater against wind waves, but little can be done if a heavy swell is present to alleviate the ship's own movement and the consequent action of a boat suspended from davits.

The first decision to be taken, when it is confirmed that a boat must be sent away, is the side on which to launch. If the vessel is stopped and lying with the wind and sea on one beam or broad on the bow, the usual choice is to lower the leeward boat, but should the ship be drifting quickly downwind then thought must be given to using the windward side as the upwelling of water from under the vessel has the effect of quelling the waves within several feet of the ship's side. In vessels where the boat deck is quite high, the length of the falls can allow the boat a large arc of swing. Should the falls be accessible from a lower deck, a wire or hook should be passed around them to bowse them to the ship thus reducing the length of the pendulum. Similarly the painter should be lead well forward, tended, and kept tight. The moment of launching should be just prior to the passage of a wave crest, in order that the falls will slacken and can be released as the next crest passes.

Ships which have a requirement to send boats away frequently, will often fit a disengaging gear (such as Robinson's) to facilitate the moment of launching. It is envisaged that the next generation of merchant ships' lifeboats will have a similar system but might also be capable of being launched and recovered while the ship is underway. The controls for lowering these boats will be in the boat itself, thus if the ship is being abandoned no one has to stay aboard as launching crew.

The recovery of a boat in a seaway also presents some problems, the initial one being the dangers associated with the falls because these may well be swinging wildly despite making a lee and 'shortening' them if possible. The dangers are threefold:

1. the heavy lower blocks may cause serious injury during the hooking on;
2. the falls may have twisted which will take time to sort out;
3. the initial shock of hoisting may cause serious damage if a wave snatches the boat.

The use of nylon pendants between the lower block and lifting hook will enable the boat to be hoisted in board where it can be slung from the davit heads while the falls are restored to their normal state.

Transfer of Personnel. It is occasionally necessary to transfer people from one vessel to another or to the shore and, depending on the circumstances, there are several methods available. In calm waters the easiest option may well be to go alongside; if this is not possible then the lowering of a boat will provide a ferry. Such conditions suggest the use of inflatable or semi-inflatable craft as their launching, recovery and sea-keeping properties are ideally suited. These craft, and particularly their engines, require thorough and regular maintenance.

Transfer is often by helicopter—indeed the harbour pilot joins by this method in some ports. From the shiphandling point of view, the principal objective is to give the helicopter pilot the best possible view of the deck area, which is marked out for helicopter operations. As a helicopter pilot traditionally sits on the starboard side of his flight deck, his best view is of the ship's deck forward of him as he comes to the hover. Because their mode of operation is suited to flying into the 'apparent' wind, the best attitude the ship can adopt is a steady course and speed with the wind thirty degrees on the port bow (Fig. 3.8).

In smaller vessels it may not be possible for the aircraft to hold station over the ship herself for fear of fouling the masts or rigging in which case an injured person might be lifted more safely from a raft or boat towed

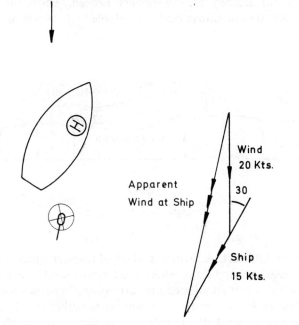

Wind
20 Kts.

Apparent
Wind at Ship

30

Ship
15 Kts.

Fig. 3.8

Working with a helicopter

astern. Those working on deck for the transfer should remember not to handle the wire until it has been earthed to remove any charge of static electricity, and *not to make the wire fast* or allow it to become fouled. Many large vessels are now being equipped with purpose built landing pads or helicopter working areas in addition to radios with a common working frequency which aids identification and communication.

Jackstay Transfers. Personnel transfer between naval vessels and their auxiliaries has often been made by jackstay. This is an extremely efficient method of transporting men or light loads from one ship to another. The basic method is for one ship, often the smaller or more manoeuvrable, to take station on one side of the other at a distance of about thirty-five to forty metres (Fig. 3.9). A line is then passed by costing gun or line throwing equipment followed by a messenger and in turn a manilla hawser. This hawser is secured in board on one ship and kept tight manually on the other. A snatch block and whip are then passed. After testing the system with a suitable (inanimate) object, personnel can be transported across. This type of transfer has two major drawbacks, firstly the high degree of skill required in station keeping and secondly the numerous trained crew members needed. Unfortunately, these requirements are not always readily available in the world of commercial shipping.

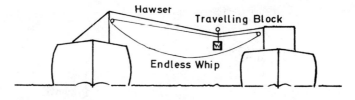

Fig.3.9

Light jackstay rig

Transfer by Life-raft. A further method of transfer which has been well tried in weather conditions where rigid boats would be dangerous to handle, is the use of an inflated life-raft; having bent on a long line to its towing becket, it is streamed down wind to the other vessel which is hove to leeward (Fig. 3.10). If the raft used is part of the ship's life saving appliances, it should be kept inflated on recovery and carefully dried before sending it to an approved servicing agent at the next suitable port for repacking and recertification.

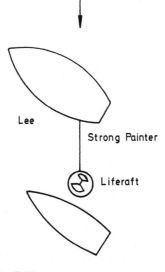

Lee

Strong Painter

 Liferaft

Fig.3.10

Transfer by Liferaft

Search Patterns. It is not infrequent for ships to be in receipt of distress messages and close enough to render assistance in the search for survivors. Such a search by one or more vessels will be far more effective if organised and controlled in a seamanlike manner. For this purpose the Inter-governmental Maritime Consultative Organisation (IMCO) have produced a book entitled the Merchant Ship Search and Rescue Manual (MERSAR) which contains the basic details necessary for the planning, organisation and execution of an SAR operation, including details of the search patterns to employ in various circumstances.

Station Keeping. When engaged in a search or under certain circumstances such as sailing in convoy, it is necessary to keep station on other vessels. By far the easiest means is to use radar if this is possible. It must be remembered, however, that in military situations radar transmissions are detectable by the opposition. It might not therefore be prudent to use such equipment as it could attract unwanted attention.

Where radar is available, the bearing cursor and range marker are set to intersect at the vessel on which station is being kept. If other means are to be used then a vertical sextant angle, say between the water line and mast head of adjacent ships, is perhaps the most efficient method. The angle to be set is obtained from the Distance off Table in any book of

45

Nautical Tables. Should the distance between ships decrease then the sextant angle will increase and appropriate action can be taken.

When turns and wheels of a convoy are made it is important that clocks are synchronised and the executive signal for all manoeuvres given by a signal from the senior vessel. So long as all involved have clear instructions as to the timing and nature of manoeuvre, and carefully monitor its execution, then such exercises in close company are orderly and safe.

Replenishment and Transfers at Sea. Both military and civilian ships engage in the transfer of fuel, stores or other cargo while they are at sea. The military have developed the techniques of replenishment underway to a high degree, enabling multiple transfer of fuel, stores and ammunition to be conducted simultaneously by hose, heavy jackstay and helicopter. Such operations are the result of many years of development and training, but the basic principles are easily understood and little or no extra equipment is required in a merchant ship to take oil from a replenishment tanker.

If a replenishment is to be made it is usual to agree to the general details of the transfer by radio beforehand. From the shiphandling aspect the important details include the course and speed to be adopted by the guide (usually the larger vessel) on whom the manoeuvring vessel is to keep station. If there is a sea running the best course to adopt is one with the weather about ten degrees on the bow of the non-operational side of the guide. The speed should be such that both vessels have full control of their manoeuvring capabilities. This might well be a speed in excess of twelve knots and as the operation can take several hours, adequate sea room should be allowed.

As was seen in Chapter 1, there are areas of positive and negative pressure around the ship's hull as she moves through the water. It is fundamental that during a transfer the two ships steam on parallel courses with sufficient distance between them that the lateral attractive force is not strong enough to overcome their resistance to this sideways movement. The critical stages are when the pressure zones are out of phase. This will occur during the approach to the guide and its effect must be anticipated. So long as the speed of approach from about twenty degrees on the guide's quarter is maintained, and corrective helm applied, the manoeuvring ship will safely pass through the zone where her bow negative area is level with the similar area at the guide's stern and she can take up station preparatory to the transfer.

A particularly dangerous situation arises if the manoeuvring ship overshoots and sheers under the guide's bow. In these circumstances it becomes impossible to accelerate out of trouble because of loss of propeller efficiency in the broken streamlines. The best action is to reduce speed immediately and risk a minor collision with the guide rather than be run down.

Once settled on a parallel course and engine revolutions are such as to keep abreast the guide's replenishment point, a costing line can be sent over and the transfer begun. One of the first lines to be sent over is a *distance line* which is taken forward so that it is clearly visible from both ships' bridges. This line is marked at regular intervals with coloured tallies enabling the manoeuvring ship to keep a constant check on the distance being maintained between the two ships. When the transfer is completed the manoeuvring ship should, when all lines are clear, steer easily away. A violent breakaway could result in a loss of speed and a collision of sterns. It is imperative that throughout the operation the compass heading being steered by the helmsmen in both vessels is monitored vigilantly, for should a lapse of concentration or a compass failure occur this can result in a potentially very dangerous situation.

Lightening transfers between VLCC's and smaller tankers are frequently made at anchor. Those tankers regularly used for lightening are equipped with large pneumatic fenders which keep the vessels safely apart in moderate sea conditions. It is the smaller tanker which usually manoeuvres alongside the larger, the VLCC having previously anchored in a suitable deep water bay offering some shelter from prevailing winds. Great care must be taken when coming together as a collision could cause massive pollution, a fire or both. It is, therefore, preferable for the lightening ship to come to rest parallel to the VLCC some fifty metres away before using air-powered costing guns to pass light lines, messengers and the mooring ropes prior to heaving alongside.

An alternative and perhaps more common method of berthing is for the VLCC to steam at about four or five knots on a course chosen by the lightening ship. The latter is then secured alongside the VLCC while underway and the transfer is made after either anchoring the larger vessel or, if weather and sea room allow, by drifting.

Note. Helicopter transfers: There is at present no international code of practice for working with helicopters. One method is quoted in this chapter, however authorities differ, particularly with respect to ship's course and the approach angle of the helicopter.

Chapter 4
Shiphandling in Heavy Weather

The Effect of Heavy Sea

The form and development of wave trains has been referred to in the previous chapter and it will be recalled that waves can become unstable and break. When breaking occurs a great mass of water surges forward and downwards from the crest. It is this weight of water coming from a breaking wave, or a wave broken by contact with the ship, which causes damage, particularly to decks and superstructures, possibly causing flooding and eventual foundering. These waves can cause immense damage even on the largest vessels where, because of their own great bulk major deck fittings can be torn from the forecastle without being immediately noticed from the bridge.

Apart from direct damage by the sea, many ships founder because their cargo has shifted due to the motion caused by the waves. The ship's movement is related to her own stability, hull form, speed and attitude to the waves in addition to the characteristics of the waves themselves.

When in a storm, therefore, the objectives, to avoid damage to ship, cargo and above all personnel, are two-fold. They are firstly to adopt a course and speed to prevent heavy waves from breaking over the decks and secondly to minimise, so far as possible, the movement of the ship. The greatest danger of all when a vessel is moving in a seaway exists when the ship's rythmic movements coincide with the apparent period of the waves. This phenomenon is called *synchronism* and will result in the angle of roll or pitch becoming very large and grave risk of cargo shifting or even machinery breaking away from its mountings.

The period of roll or pitch is the time taken for a complete movement in that plane, for example a roll from port to starboard and back to port again, whereas the *apparent period* of the waves, or *period of encounter* as it is sometimes known, is the time taken for the passage of successive wave crests as seen by a ship borne observer. In a following sea this period will, therefore, be longer than in a head sea as it takes account of the ship's own speed through the water.

A ship's natural period of roll or pitch varies with her degree of stability, a stiff ship rolling more quickly than a tender one, and a ship with her ends heavily loaded pitching sluggishly by comparison with one which has plenty of reserve buoyancy in her ends.

If synchronism occurs, or is likely to occur, an alteration of course or speed will destroy the sequence. However if the vessel is broken down she will be very vulnerable to synchronous rolling and means must be found to alter the angle that the hull makes with the waves. In smaller vessels the use of steadying sails or sea anchors are the traditional methods of bringing the ship's head up to meet the oncoming seas.

High Winds

As noted earlier, wind is the principal cause of waves, the effect of which has already been discussed, but very strong winds can also present a threat to the ship's safety whether a high sea is running or not. Some of these effects, particularly those relating to vessels hove to, were discussed in Chapter 1. If the wind strength is high enough in relation to the ship's own power she may well start to fall from her course, or alternatively refuse to come up to it. This will result in the ship steaming in the often more dangerous beam-on mode, and making a great deal of leeway. Under such circumstances the loss of ground to leeward could be extremely high, perhaps at a rate of 2 knots with a further increment of up to 6 knots due to drift current if the wind has prevailed for some time. The dreaded presence of a lee shore must always be allowed for at the voyage planning stage.

Steaming into a Head Sea

The factors to be considered here are:

1. The force of the waves on the bows causing *panting* and *pounding* stresses on the plating and forepart;
2. The *hogging* and *sagging* stresses as the ship moves through the wave crests;
3. The impact of waves breaking over the hull due to its own speed through the water or pitching into the seas.

Considering the last of these, there have been many examples of loaded tankers (usually the larger ones) ploughing into head seas and doing considerable damage to forecastle deck fittings where, because of their own great mass, the impact of these waves was not felt in the accommodation or on the bridge. One such incident caused flooding of the forward pump room and dry cargo hatch and necessitated returning to port for shelter and repairs.

It must be remembered that the impact forces increase with the product of the ship's mass and the square of the combined velocities of ship and waves. The effect of a speed reduction can thus be readily appreciated and in large vessels such reductions should be made for tabulated wind speeds in open sea, regardless of whether or not the impact of the breaking waves is physically noticeable.

Hogging and *sagging* are caused when the ship is alternately supported by waves at her ends and then by a single crest amidships (Fig. 4.1). If the condition becomes serious, permanent structural damage may be done, such as cracking of the sheer strake and ship's side plating—indeed ships have been known to break in two under such circumstances. Bad loading will exacerbate hogging and sagging stresses. The best way to counter severe bending moments of this type is to put the seas wide on the bow which lengthens the part of the hull supported by each wave.

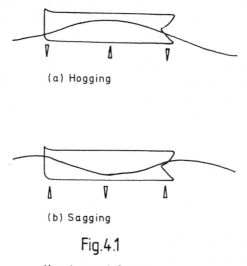

(a) Hogging

(b) Sagging

Fig.4.1

Hogging and Sagging

Panting and *pounding* stresses are an expected part of a ship's life and the scantlings around the bow and stern are increased for this reason. When pitching becomes violent the whole forefoot lifts clear of the surface and slams down again. In such conditions severe structural damage can result and steps should be taken to reduce the slamming by a course alteration, altering the trim if well by the stern or a speed alteration.

Steaming with the Seas Abeam

In this attitude rolling is the major danger, pitching being minimal. Should the rolling lead towards synchronism then an immediate course alteration should be made to alter the relationship.

The other major danger in heavy rolling is that of cargo and fittings shifting, leading to the vessel taking a list and eventually capsizing. When rolling becomes heavy serious thought should be given to heaving to. The angle of roll might not be great on a stiff ship, but the force acting to dislodge cargo can be greater than that found in a tender vessel moving through a large angle of roll.

In vessels equipped with stabilisers designed to smooth out the rolling movement of the ship in a seaway, it must be remembered that these are susceptible to mechanical failure and this is most likely to occur at the time of greatest stress. The temptation to reduce or neglect cargo lashings because stabilisers are part of the ship's equipment must therefore be strongly resisted.

Heavy Following Seas

When seas are abaft the beam two further dangers face the mariner, namely *broaching to* and *being pooped*. Broaching to occurs when the waves are travelling at or about the same speed as the ship. If the wave is large enough, in relation to the vessel, she may develop the tendency when on the down slopes to gain momentum and, in small craft particularly, to start *surfing*. This is acceptable so long as steering can be maintained but should the rudder stall then there is a grave risk of the bows digging in to the trough and a violent uncontrollable sheer developing. This causes the craft to slew at right angles to her original direction and roll heavily to leeward, at the mercy of the wave she has just slid down.

These circumstances can be avoided in several ways. The primary one must, as always, be to anticipate the situation and, if the following seas increase in size, to turn to a safer course before they become a threat. When in a following sea the qualities of the helmsman are tested and he must take action to avoid a sheer before it develops. Smaller craft can be given a great deal of stability when stern to the sea by trailing bights of rope astern which correct any inclination of the stern to overtake the bow. Finally, the ship's own strength will help to preserve her, with her stability and seaworthiness to resist the forces of a knockdown, free herself from the waves and adopt a safe heading before being pounded again.

Pooping happens when the waves are overtaking the ship and break

51

over the after deck. It is a special danger in ships with low freeboard aft or those having stern doors and ramps. Rig supply vessels face considerable danger in such circumstances and must, if carrying a cargo of pipes for example, allow sufficient stability not only for the weight of cargo but also for the weight of water which could instantaneously be trapped in those pipes causing a capsizing moment. To prevent swamping, the closing of hatches and watertight doors must be attended to with great care; there are several cases on record of trawlers, ferries and supply ships having been lost when a pooping wave has poured down an open or damaged hatch.

Of these two dangers pooping is probably the lesser and thus speed should be adjusted to well below that of the waves but sufficient to maintain steerage way.

With the sea further round on the quarter, rolling is often at its worst, and a fair degree of pitching is also present. This increase in rolling is partially caused by steering difficulties leading to yawing and then the ship will, on occasion, meet a wave so increasing the rolling force.

Heaving To

The prudent mariner will, when sea room allows, heave to in a high sea in order to avoid unnecessary punishment. The most usual method of heaving to is to choose a heading with the wind two to four points on the port bow and adjust the speed to maintain bare steerage way. The exact angle off the wind must be ascertained by trial and error to find a suitable mean between the possible damage to the ship's longitudinal structure due to pitching, the threat of cargo moving in heavy rolling, the ability of the ship to steer in the conditions and the period of duration of encounter. The reason for putting the port bow into the sea is that conventionally the transverse thrust of the propeller will assist in pointing the head into the wind. If the distance between the ship and the storm centre can be increased by having the sea on the starboard bow this might well be the better choice.

A second method of heaving to is with the sea abaft the beam. This requires ample sea room but if it takes the ship towards calmer waters and towards her destination if may be a good choice. Pitching will be reduced but rolling might well be increased and the ship's steering qualities must be sufficient to control violent yawing and prevent pooping or broaching. A further danger in a ship which is 'flying light' is that the rudder and propeller may be damaged by the breaking sea slamming into them.

The third alternative is for the vessel to 'lie ahull' or beam on to the sea. If this attitude is adopted voluntarily then the dangers of synchronism must be countered by using the engines to power the ship out of a threatening sequence of rolling. Again a lot of leeway will be made but perhaps less than when hove to with the sea on the quarter. Rolling will be heavy in this position but it is unlikely that there will be much longitudinal movement. When being hove to is involuntary, as in the case of an engine breakdown, the ship will then take up her natural angle to the sea for her draft and trim.

If the effects of synchronism becomes apparent then urgent measures must be taken to try to alter the rolling/encounter relationship. Fortunately, the largest ships are tankers and because of their internal subdivisions, cargo shifting is not a threat. In smaller ships, of higher freeboard, it may be possible to stream a sea anchor to break the harmony between rolling period and period of encounter.

Turning in a Seaway

A ship's turning circle is smaller and slightly quicker when performed at low speed with bursts or 'kicks' of the propeller to cause the rudder to bite. It is this method of turning which is best employed if it is necessary to turn from being hove to head to sea to running before it, or vice-versa. The major judgement is the timing of the turn. As explained earlier when considering the general pattern of waves, they tend to travel in alternately increasing and decreasing amplitudes resulting in times of relative calm. It is these calm periods which should be utilised to the maximum benefit.

When turning from having the seas ahead to put them astern, the manoeuvre should be timed so that the calm period of the cycle coincides with the ship being beam on to the swell. In other words the calm must be anticipated in order to reduce the risk of a knockdown in a heavy beam sea.

The reverse turn, from running before the storm to bringing it ahead requires even greater anticipation as the last half of the turn needs to be completed in the calm. This is because in low powered ships and those with a large freeboard, it may be difficult to bring them up into the wind and thus the calm period should be used to try to steer the vessel head to wind without being stopped by the heavier seas.

Weather Routeing

The preceding sections of this chapter have considered possible courses of action when in heavy weather. The best action, however, is to avoid, so far as possible, the chance of encountering adverse conditions. There are two possible ways of solving this problem, firstly by providing the shipmaster with sufficient information to make on-board decisions and secondly by providing advice on routeing from a shore station.

It has been recognised for many years that, from a statistical point of view, one route will be favoured above others at a particular season of the year. These routes, which appear in such publications as *Ocean Passages* and pilot charts, are based on meteorological and oceanographical data, including ice information, collected over many years. Traditionally ships have followed these routes to take the benefit of ocean currents and prevailing winds but, although they reduce the chances of meeting inclement conditions, modern communications systems offer more up-to-date intelligence on the whereabouts of hostile weather systems.

As has been explained earlier the ship's performance in a seaway depends on her own dimensions, available power and handling characteristics. Related to these factors are such parameters as fuel consumption, cargo damage, crew and passenger safety, damage to the ship and maintenance of schedules. The navigator's task, therefore, is not simply to take his ship directly from A to B but to take it safely along the route giving the best economic return to his principals.

If the routeing decisions are to be made on board, the master and navigating officers must have a thorough knowledge of basic meteorology and have at their disposal up-to-date synoptic and prognostic charts of weather systems and wave patterns. Facsimile machines are available which enable this information to be recorded on the ship's bridge. The master is then able to make his own routeing plans and keep them updated from information available on board.

The alternative to this method is to use expert advice provided from a shore-based establishment which has been informed of the ship's response to various conditions, especially wave fields. Having been advised of her points of departure and destination, the service will provide regular communications to suggest variations of course which will try to achieve a previously stated objective. These objectives could be: the least time passage; the least time with least damage to hull and cargo; the least damage; maintenance of a scheduled speed; minimum fuel cost. Savings such as these can be considerable when taken over a fleet year and compared to the modest cost of the routeing charges.

However, these shore and ship based systems are not infallible and thus the mariner must be prepared to handle his ship in adverse conditions. Indeed, although maximum flexibility exists in mid-ocean, there is little that can be done to avoid bad weather if committed to fixed schedules at the termini. Nevertheless such methods, when tempered with the mariner's experience, do offer improved voyage performance which should benefit all with an interest in the venture.

Tropical Revolving Storms

One of the hazards facing the seafarer in the otherwise quite pleasant and meteorologically tame sub-tropical latitudes, is the tropical revolving storm (TRS) or as they are referred to locally, the hurricane, typhoon, cyclone and willy-willy.

These areas of intense low pressure apparently originate in the proximity of island groups in low latitudes, and after following a basically westward path will often recurve to the north and east on reaching latitudes of between 20° and 30° in the northern hemisphere—somewhat lower in the southern hemisphere. Within 75 miles of the centre the wind is frequently found to be more violent than in a depression of higher latitude, and because of the rapidity of movement of the system, the sea state becomes very confused.

The areas of the world where TRS's are found and their seasons are well known, and the mariner should pay attention to the radio for early warning and also carefully monitor his own meteorological observations for the tell-tale signs. These are, briefly, a fall in barometric pressure several millibars below the corrected diurnal range, an unexplained swell, extensive cirrus cloud development, threatening sky and increasing wind.

If a storm is anticipated the wise seaman will take avoiding action after determining the bearing of the storm centre and its path. The rules for plotting this information may be found in meteorological texts, the *Mariners Handbook* and the *Sailing Directions* (pilot books), but it is worth pointing out that early action, when the ship is not suffering any restriction of movement, is infinitely preferable to trying to ride out such a storm.

Icing

In blizzard conditions or when taking spray with the air temperature below −2°C (the freezing temperature of sea water) there is a grave risk of ice forming on decks, superstructures and rigging. This addition of top weight can be extremely detrimental to the ship's statical stability. Ice accumulation may originate in three ways:

1. Freezing fog;
2. Freezing rain and drizzle;

3. Sea spray or water breaking over the ship and being frozen in the cold air.

If the ship is headed into the sea and thus taking heavy spray and water there will be a temptation to turn and run before the storm to reduce icing. However, this manoeuvre must not be attempted unless absolutely sure of the positive stability of the ship, as any loss, in addition to the normal dangers of turning in a heavy sea, might prove fatal. Several trawler losses have been attributed to capsizes under severe icing. The only apparent means of ridding the ship of this unwanted weight is by axe and crow bar but care should be taken to avoid injury from ice falling from aloft.

Quelling Seas with Oil

A film of oil on the sea surface will tend to prevent wave crests from breaking and thus reduce the amount of water and spray coming aboard. The swell waves will not be affected but a lessening of the wind waves may be of benefit in reducing icing or working with a small craft. Thin vegetable or animal oils should preferably be used and in cold weather they may be thinned by a spirit or by warming. Mineral oils should not be used when there is a possibility of harming persons in the water, but if all else fails lubricating oil can be tried.

The method of distribution is to allow the oil to seep slowly out of a porous bag, or through the scuppers and overboard discharges on the windward side of the vessel. A spar might be run out to carry the oil over the side. A rate of flow of under ten litres per hour is sufficient to give the maximum aid.

Sea Anchors and Drogues

In smaller vessels it can be beneficial to steady the movement on a seaway by using some form of external device to assist in maintaining a suitable attitude to the wind and sea. The principle is that an object with no windage is streamed over the bow and the boat will then drift down wind of this sea anchor (Fig. 4.2).

The form of sea anchor used could be one of the purpose built types which are fitted into life-boats and rafts or, in larger ships, a bight of mooring rope may help when disabled and lying in a heavy beam sea. Some yachts run well before a storm under storm jib and a bight of rope streamed over the stern, and this method has the advantage that the scope of the bight can be altered to suit the conditions. The standard

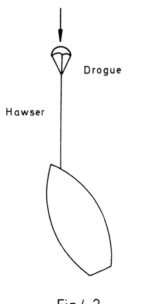

Fig.4.2

Principle of the sea anchor

pattern of sea anchor has the major disadvantage that the warp and tripping line can become badly twisted making recovery very difficult. If recovery is not required then the tripping line can be dispensed with.

The limiting size of ship which can stream a drogue is not as small as is sometimes thought. For example survey vessels of over three thousand tons have lain for days to an ex-army parachute streamed on the end of a mooring rope. It may not be possible to recover such gear but its cost is small compared with the damage which could be caused by rolling in the seaway.

By using anchors and anchor cables it is also possible to bring the vessel head to wind in deep water. The method employed is to walk the anchors out so that several shackles are in the water. The additional drag at the bow will cause the stern to fall off down wind. In shallower waters dredging three shackles of cable on the bottom will have a similar effect. The cable is broken at a joining link on deck and led through the forward ring or fairlead after lashing the anchor in the hawse pipe. Should the cable foul a submerged object, it should be buoyed and then slipped for later recovery.

Stranding on a Lee Shore

Being blown onto a lee shore is always a danger, particularly in ships which are low powered or light draft. There are several remedies which may be attempted, to assist the vessel in making some ground to windward. The first is to try to give the propeller and rudder more bite by taking on ballast. This is relatively easy in a tanker but may require the flooding of lower holds or deep tanks in dry cargo ships.

Other options include *wearing about* by running down wind to gather sufficient way before attempting to turn head to wind and steam off the lee shore. The danger here is that valuable sea room is lost which may not be recovered. Another means of turning the ship to the sea is to snub an anchor on the bottom and weigh it as headway is gathered. Lastly remember the old dictum: 'never go aground with your anchors in the pipes'. They might hold and are therefore worth trying if all else has failed.

Freak Waves

The popular press has in recent years made much of so called 'freak waves'. However, there is evidence to support the theory that in certain parts of the world waves can occur, due to a combination of factors, which are big enough to overwhelm or severely damage quite large ships. Over a period of years the area of sea to the east of South Africa has gained some notoriety in this context, as has an area to the south of Norway, though to a lesser extent.

It is thought that the cause of waves building to these heights is not attributable to the wind alone but is due to a strong ocean current meeting a heavy wave train and perhaps to some effect from reducing soundings. Should conditions occur which allow a larger wave to develop, through resonance between difference wave trains, and this large wave becomes unstable and breaks, a ship meeting it at that instant would be likely to suffer heavy damage if not capsized by falling into the trough.

Statistically one wave in 300,000 will be four times the average wave height and the highest wave recorded by instruments is 25 metres. The remedy therefore is to use routeing systems to avoid wave trains and the areas where danger is known to exist when a heavy swell is running.

Chapter 5
Aids to Mooring — Ropes and Cables

The purpose of ropes and wires aboard ship goes further than merely trussing the vessel alongside a quay wall when in port. Used properly they are valuable aids to shiphandling when manoeuvring in restricted waters and on approaching and leaving berths. They may be used as 'levers' around which a ship can be turned and as 'brakes' to check the way which a ship is making. The proper use of a 'spring' when bringing a ship off a wall is an extremely efficient way of using the available forces. However, before the techniques of using wires and ropes are discussed, the properties of these materials should be examined.

The Properties of Fibre Ropes

The features which different materials can offer when used in rope construction are: *flexibility*, *strength*, *elasticity*; and from the negative aspect: *breaking strain*, *bulk*, *melting temperature* and *behaviour when wet*. Perhaps the most important factor after these basic requirements have been met is that the rope should handle well. Traditionally, cordage was made of vegetable fibres laid up to form ropes of vastly differing specifications. Consider the difference between the rope used for a lead line, which had to be free of stretch and resistant to kinking, and a heavy coir spring, used to damp the ranging of ships secured alongside, often in ports subject to a heavy swell where bulk and a degree of elasticity are required. Manila and sisal were used for the construction of mooring ropes, the usual form being hawser lay. In recent years synthetic fibres have replaced them largely because their resistance to natural decay gave them a longer life and hence, assuming a similar initial cost, offered a financial saving.

Natural fibres have many advantages, the principal ones being ease of handling (except when wet or frozen), audible warning before parting and reliable behaviour when under tension. When wet they tend to become very stiff and if this water freezes the rope becomes unmanageable. Synthetic ropes on the other hand do not absorb water into their fibres and, size for size, have greater strength than their natural equivalent. This strength can, with some of the materials used (polyester, polyamide and polypropylene, for example) mean that the fibre ropes are stronger than the wire ropes aboard the ship.

Despite these advantages of strength and durability, synthetic fibre ropes have some unpleasant characteristics. They give little warning of parting and because they can have very elastic properties this causes a considerable back lash. As with many plastics their properties change with temperature, thus frictional heat around a bad lead or winch drum can cause melting and fusion, with the dangers associated with such weakening. Likewise, because the method of production requires extrusion from a nozzle giving continuous plastic fibres, many ropes have a smooth finish which leads to difficult handling. It has been necessary to cut these continuous fibres to spin yarns similar to those found in manila and sisal ropes, to produce ropes which can be safely worked in the marine environment. The latter type of rope is referred to as staple, whereas those having continuous fibres are either mono or multi-filament.

Elasticity, as mentioned above, is a feature of some types of synthetics relative to natural fibre rope. *Polyamide* (often known by the trade name Nylon) is very elastic and can be stretched to half its length again without losing its original form. Thus, despite its great strength, it would be unsuitable as a mooring rope but well suited to use as a tail joined to a towing wire, where its elasticity would make an ideal shock absorber. *Polyester* (often called by the trade name Terylene) has relatively little stretch and is also strong. However, its cost is high and it tends to be used for specialist purposes only. The synthetic fibre used most for marine ropes in general purpose tasks, including mooring, is *polypropylene*.

Another way of altering the characteristics of a rope is to use different types of lay or method of twisting the strands together. Traditionally, mooring ropes would be of *hawser lay*, which is three strands laid up right-handed or clockwise. Such a rope was prone to 'kinking' if not coiled down properly, i.e. in the direction of the lay. The tightness of the twist would also affect the degree of flexibility a rope might have. Many contemporary ropes are of *plaited lay*, which is far more forgiving so far as kinking is concerned and is flexible for easy handling. Plaited polypropylene is perhaps the most common rope in use for mooring today.

The Care of Fibre Ropes

The characteristics of fibre ropes vary a great deal, particularly in respect to the chemical properties of the synthetics. Some are resistant to acids, some to alkalis and some will not deteriorate if in contact with oil. Natural fibre ropes will rot and this is particularly so if stored wet or in a damp place. It is perhaps better then, to lay down a general rule for the care of mooring ropes rather than try to remember a series of chemical reactions. This rule must then be to avoid contact with any type of oil or chemical and to stow ropes on gratings in well aired spaces. Additionally, some types of synthetic fibre suffer from actinic degradation if exposed to the sun's rays. It is therefore prudent to stow ropes in the shade or to cover them with tarpaulins when not in use. Contact with ferrous metal also causes rapid deterioration if any rusting is present. The stowage on gratings or pallets helps in this respect too.

When in use a rope should never be subjected to excessive strain as, in addition to the risks associated with breaking, it may be permanently 'crippled' and weakened. Passing ropes around in sharp bights tends to open up the lay and thus cause an effective loss of strength. Care should be taken to avoid chafing, particularly when wires are used in addition to fibre ropes, as the wires will tend to perform a sawing action as the ship ranges up and down. It is good policy to run two ropes ashore in quick succession as this will halve the strain when heaving alongside and enable the tension to be held on one while the other is being secured to the bitts. To avoid unnecessary frictional heat all rollers should be free moving and warping drums should be smooth and free from rust. For safety when heaving on synthetic ropes on a 'non-whelped' drum no more than three turns should normally be used to avoid heat and binding around the drum. The person handling the rope on the drum should be backed up by a second whose task it is to coil the rope clear of the working area. This part of the deck should be non-slip and the controls of the winch or capstan should be constantly within the reach of a competent seaman who should have no other duties.

When two ropes are to be put on the same bollard ashore it is usual to 'dip' the eyes of the second and bring it up through the eye of the first, thus enabling them to be let go in any order without disturbing the other ropes on that post. This is important if ropes are from another ship and she is to sail first. Generally, the material used for rope stoppers should be the same as that used in the lay up of the rope it is to hold, with the exception that polyamide (Nylon) is not used for stoppers, because of its elasticity.

The Properties of Wire Rope and its Care

Staple fibre ropes tend to have their strength in the frictional forces which hold the fibres together when laid up. Filament ropes and wire ropes, however, gain their strength from the continuous nature of the extrusions from which they are made. Wire ropes in marine use are often constructed out of six strands of wire laid up right-handed around a core or heart. However, a noticeable increase in special plaited lays has occurred since cranes became a more frequently found feature of a ship's outfit.

The heart of a general purpose wire rope would be made of natural fibre, jute or hemp being preferred. The purpose of this heart, in addition to providing a former around which to construct the rope, is to act as a reservoir for the lubricant and as a shock absorber. The application of grease or oil to all working wires is essential to ensure that oxidisation of the steel is avoided, and to enable the wires within the strands to move freely against each other to help promote flexibility. Flexibility can also be varied by controlling the number of wires per strand. Standing rigging, for example, has few wires in a strand whereas special highly flexible types may have over sixty wires in each strand. The safest and best stowage for wires is on reels. These can be kept covered at sea to help preserve them, but when about to be used for mooring, wires should be run off their reels and flaked out up and down the deck. It is dangerous practice to run a wire directly off a reel because of the risk of the reel jamming under strain and tearing free of its mounting.

Chain stoppers are used for relieving tension on wire ropes during the working of the heaving part. Two well spaced half hitches, in the form of a 'cow' hitch, should be backed up by laying the remaining chain up around the wire, the stopper's end being held by a rope lanyard.

Handling wire rope is not without its difficulties as a wire is far more resistant to being coiled against its direction of lay than a fibre rope. The golden rule is that a wire should never be forced against its 'will' and when coiling it down it is necessary to reverse many of the turns to avoid kinking which would severely cripple the wire and render it unsafe. Occasionally individual wires in a strand can break and stick out of the rope as a 'snag'. These can be dangerous to handlers and if too many are broken the strength of the rope is impaired and it should be condemned.

Wire rope is relatively inelastic and if excessive strain is applied tends to 'strand' rather than part in one break. However, if subject to sudden breaking they may lash about and cause serious injury to anyone close by.

Typical Mooring Plans

The traditional method of securing a ship alongside is by a combination of ropes and wires, the arrangement aft being a reflection of that used forward. As shown in Fig. 5.1 the plan consists of those ropes which lead fore and aft to arrest any movement along the quay and others secured at right angles to the fore and aft line to stop movement away from the quay. The ropes leading forward or aft of the ship from it's extremities are usually referred to as *head ropes* (from the forecastle) or *stern ropes* (from the poop). Those leading fore and aft but in a direction towards amidships, that is from the forecastle leading aft and from the poop or afterdeck leading forward are known as *springs*. A rope lead abeam is a *breastrope*.

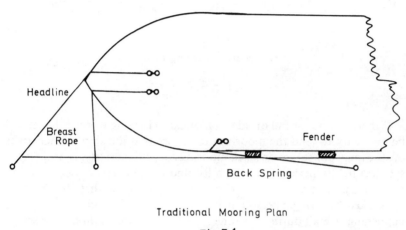

Traditional Mooring Plan

Fig.5.1

A properly secured ship will lie firmly alongside with the keel parallel to the berth. There should be equal stress in all the ropes. Fibre ropes are commonly used as head, stern and breastropes whereas wires are often used as springs. It is quite normal for three or four head or stern ropes to be used, two from each bow or quarter, single parts being used else-where. If strong tidal streams or winds are expected or engine trials or a long stay in port are planned then the above moorings should be 'doubled', by running additional ends or bights of rope or wire.

Variations of the above systems are frequent as the construction of the berth may make a departure from the ideal necessary. Breastropes, for example, should not be used if the lead is steep as the force will tend to act vertically instead of horizontally. As crew sizes become smaller, labour saving systems of mooring have been devised as shown in Fig. 5.2. Only fibre ropes are used with two lead forward and two lead aft at each end of the vessel.

63

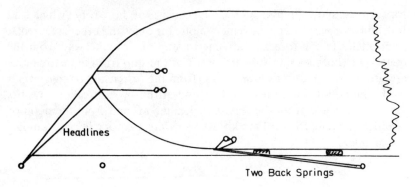

Alternative Mooring Plan

Fig.5.2

If there is a rise or fall of tide and/or cargo is being worked then it will be necessary to tend the moorings to ensure that the ship neither drifts off the quay nor surges on slack moorings or, alternatively, is held alongside too tightly perhaps causing a list and the parting of ropes. An important aspect of safety when tending moorings is that they should never be worked by a single person as it is not possible for him to see what is happening overall during the time his concentration is directed towards some particular task, such as easing a rope.

Winches Capstans and Self-tensioning Winches

The properties of these machines are equally as important to the ship-handler as a knowledge of the ropes, wires and cables used in securing the ship. This is particularly the case when arriving at or leaving a berth or mooring under adverse conditions, and the need arises to use the equipment to the safe limits of speed and tension.

The principal difference between a winch and a capstan is the direction of the axis of rotation, winch barrels being horizontal and capstan's vertical. Turns of rope have to be put round the end of the drum manually and this operation can be severely hampered by lack of personnel, poor weather or strain coming on the rope before sufficient turns have been taken. The master and pilot must consider these factors when planning the arrival or departure manoeuvres.

The propulsion of these machines is by steam, electricity or hydraulic power. Steam is less fashionable nowadays though many ships are still equipped with this type of auxiliary. The important thing to remember is that steam plants must be warmed through and the cylinders drained of condensed water before they can be used. This means that manoeuvres requiring the use of the winches must be anticipated by several minutes to enable the crew to make them ready. Cold climates may cause any condensate to freeze in the pipes which can fracture cylinder blocks and pipe runs and this should be avoided, either by blowing the line through and draining before shutting down or keeping the winches turning over out of gear. The former requires very slow and careful warming prior to the next operation if the ship is still in sub-zero temperatures. The latter method, while ensuring that the machines are ready warmed for use, is extremely expensive on boiler fuel.

Electric and hydraulic winches do not suffer these difficulties but electric units may not be suitable in flammable atmospheres, and hydraulic systems have become unpopular because of the persistence of the fluid should there be a leak.

Many ships, particularly the larger ones, are fitted with self-tensioning winches on which the mooring rope is permanently coiled onto a drum. When mooring or leaving a berth they are controlled manually to pay out or heave in as required. When secured in position these winches can be left to maintain tension at a pre-determined value. As the ship rises or sinks the winch will pay out or take in slack to maintain this tension. Problems arise if an offshore wind or tidal set exerts a pressure on the ship's hull greater than the combined resistance of the winches in use, resulting in the ship being forced off her berth with no immediate means of checking a dangerous situation. For this reason it is usual to send away some ropes which are turned up on bitts in the traditional way. It has been reported that on some ships the ropes have been wound onto the winches in the wrong direction thus negating the automatic tension device.

The ropes used on these winches may well be 'combination' ropes of fibre and wire as they are less rough to handle than pure wires but retain some of the qualities of the latter to resist kinking or riding.

The Use of Springs in Manoeuvring

As mentioned above the skilful use of a spring can be of great service in canting the ship. The usual requirement is to swing the stern off the quay in order that the propeller might be safely used, or perhaps to allow a pontoon or lighters to be brought between the ship and the quay.

If it is the stern which is to be brought off then the after moorings are slackened, the forward breastrope leads to a drum end and the weight

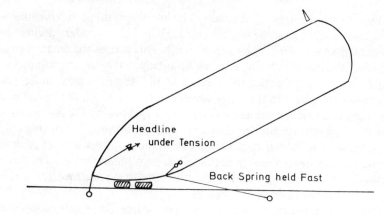

Use of a Spring to Cant the Stern Off.

Fig.5.3

taken. Having checked that the fore spring is tight and adequate, and thus preventing any advance ahead, the breastrope should be heaved easily. The bow will then be slowly brought towards the quay around the curve of the hull shape as the stern swings off (Fig. 5.3). Similarly on any occasion when there is a requirement to make no movement up or down the berth then the appropriate spring should be held to stop this movement and the breastrope at the opposite end of the ship held to check any tendency to swing off the berth. To stop ahead movement, the forward spring should be held and vice-versa to resist any force acting towards the stern.

Anchors, Cables and Cable Handling Gear

In Chapter 7 several methods of using the anchors in shiphandling are described. A conventional ship has its anchors stowed foward in hawse pipes, fitted into the ship's hull on either bow. Ships built for specific trades are sometimes fitted with stern anchors. Drilling ships, pipe-laying barges and other unconventional vessels have eight or more anchors arranged around the hull, usually joined to the ship by chain cable although heavy wires are frequently used in vessels which manoeuvre by their anchors alone (as in the case of dredgers and construction barges). This chain cable is lead over or around the gipsy of a windlass or capstan and then down the spurling pipe into the chain locker.

The majority of chain lockers found aboard modern ships are self-stowing, that is, as the cable comes down the spurling pipe it flakes itself in such a manner that it will not fall over and become entangled. Older ships had lockers in which the cable had to be stowed manually by the crew, the technique being to stand outside the locker and ease the cable into the appropriate position with wooden battens as it came aboard. It was, of course, essential to muster crew members on the upper deck before informing the bridge that the anchors were ready to let go.

Some large vessels of later designs have separate windlasses for each hawse pipe, which may be angled to achieve a more direct lead. Other types have separate windlasses capable of being coupled together when weighing anchor. Another design variation is to have the anchor lead directly over a heavy casting built into the deck edge, thus making a hawse pipe redundant.

The weight of anchors and cables in use on VLCC's and their ilk is considerable. Unfortunately, there is some history of anchoring mishaps with this size of ship, leading to the opinion that some of the gear, and indeed the anchors themselves, may not match the vessels which carry them. Similarly, a certain class of warship was built with only one anchor. The practice of good seamanship can condone neither of these faults and because of emergency situations, as well as daily operations, the ship's personnel need to rely on the effectiveness of their anchors, cables and handling equipment.

When coming to an anchor it is necessary, particularly in ships of high freeboard or bulbous bow, to 'walk' the anchor out to the water's edge before securing the brake and disengaging the gears. When ordered to let go, sufficient cable should be allowed to run out for the anchor to take the sea bed but without the cable piling up on top of it. The friction of the anchor and cable on the bottom should be sufficient to cause more cable to run out under the control of the windlass or capstan as the ship slowly makes way, ahead or astern, depending on the favoured method of anchoring.

The amount of cable to be run out before securing will have been determined prior to anchoring, taking into account the depth of water, strength of stream or current, nature and holding properties of the ground, length of stay, weight of tackle, etc. A minimum of three times the depth of water is a rule of thumb for normal anchorages, but this rule must be flexible and particularly so as the depth increases. Cable is traditionally made in *shackles* which are fifteen fathoms long, the joining links between each shackle being convenient measures for telling how much cable is out. Each join is additionally marked by painting the links and putting a couple of turns of seizing wire around the stud in the link, an appropriate number each side of the join. For example, the end of the fifth shackle would be marked by having the fifth stud link, either side of the joining link, marked as described. It is most important that the cable is re-marked and the old markings removed when the order of the shackles is re-arranged. This will be done as part of the dry docking schedule to ensure even wear of the cable. The re-marking should be superintended by one of the deck officers.

The anchors and cables require little maintenance outside being ranged at drydocking, other than to check from time to time that the markings are visible for day and night use and that the lead seals are still in position covering the ends of the spile pins in the joining links. The cable handling gear, however, requires regular attention to ensure that all bearing surfaces move freely and that the motors are fully efficient. Brake bands should be kept free of grease and oil and inspected for wear.

When letting go an anchor all personnel should move well away from the run of the cable and the person controlling the windlass should wear protective clothing including goggles. As the cable runs out the bridge should be informed of the numbers of shackles and the direction in which the cable is 'growing'. The ship is said to be *brought up* to her anchor when, having held on to the required length of cable, it slowly sinks into catenary as the weight of the cable draws the vessel ahead. A rapid sagging might well indicate that the anchor is not holding. Placing a hand on the cable will often give the 'feel' of what is happening on the sea bed.

When weighing anchor the bridge should be kept informed, as the cable comes in, of the remaining length, its direction and any excessive strains. A careful inspection must be made, as the anchor breaks surface, to ensure that no unwanted matter such as power or telephone lines or other cables are fouling the anchor. Their pressure may well have been indicated by unusual and excessive groaning of the windlass after the anchor is aweigh.

From the shiphandling point of view it is not prudent to make way in the time interval between the anchor being aweigh and being sighted if this can be avoided within other operational parameters, such as the need to stem the tidal stream.

Chapter 6
Navigation in Confined Waters

It is often said in discussion of shiphandling techniques that a certain vessel 'has a mind of her own' in a given circumstance. Evidence of this might appear overwhelming at times, but obviously must be rejected for a more rational explanation. What is certain is that there may be more than a dozen forces acting about the vessel's axes at any given moment, and that the resultant may not be as anticipated but due partially to a force which has escaped discovery. This is not 'mysticism' so much as lack of the research which takes the art of shiphandling into the finite world of applied science.

Experience of shiphandling soon teaches the 'handler' that the skills he employs must not only be sound but also flexible and capable of instant adjustment to circumstances which change continuously. There can be few absolute solutions to manoeuvring problems because only some of the variables are within the control of the shiphandler, while the external variables may alter with the differing styles of application of the controllable forces. Correct ways of solving a problem are not therefore wholly matters of fact in as much as they are too complex to be measured, and are thus subject to professional opinion.

There are, however, basic techniques which can be learned. The layman would understand them as the application of forces about a point, mechanics being the popular name for this area of physics. In the horizontal plane these forces often act about the turning centre which lies approximately one third of the length from forward, whereas changes in trim and heel will be about other centres. The ship's captain, pilot or officer have to combine this theoretical knowledge with their experience of handling vessels of varying shapes, propulsive systems and steering capabilities in differing conditions of water flow, weather and sea bed.

Local customs in technique are initially developed to overcome peculiar difficulties and then used in other circumstances because of the expertise gained. Use of the anchor in port manoeuvres is very much in this category. In ports where tugs have been a rare sight, if seen at all, the pilots become skilled in using the anchor for turning, berthing and mooring. Had tugs been available the objective would have been the same but the means of achieving it quite different, and the expertise developed would have been different.

The Ship's Variable Factors

The ship's variable factors have been discussed in Chapter 2 but a summary of these will be useful before considering specific situations. They are:

1. The size and shape—particularly in relation to the space available above and below the waterline.
2. Engine power and type—the mass to power ratio and the reaction time being important factors.
3. Steering capability—is it affected by shallow water, trim and low speed?
4. Draft and trim—the principal concern here being under keel and overhead clearances.
5. Manoeuvring aids—direct engine control, controllable pitch propellers, shipboard communications, bow and stern thrusters, steerable propellers and nozzles.
6. External aids—tugs, mooring boats, ship to ship and ship to shore communications. Also shore gang, and very short range navigational equipment, for example for giving distance off berth.

In general it can be said that the shiphandler has either direct control over these factors or will know from experience what well defined characteristics are to be expected. For many larger vessels in docks and rivers the relationship between the ship's characteristics and the prevailing physical limits is such that, even with the most careful planning, the execution of traditional shiphandling techniques is impossible and the use of tugs becomes necessary for maintaining a proper position in the channel.

The External Factors

Wind, tidal stream or current and shallow water effects have already been mentioned as being the major forces acting on the ship, over which the shiphandler has little or no influence. The drift effects of the first two are usually obvious and will vary in proportion to the windage area or draft, but although they can inhibit a manoeuvre and on occasion prevent it, they can also be used to advantage. In a confined space the difference between success and failure will lie in correctly assessing their effect as forces acting on the vessel and properly allowing for or using them. The wind may be reasonably determined as to its strength and direction whereas tidal sets and velocities are likely to vary considerably as they eddy around obstructions in a fast flowing stream. Obviously then, this knowledge must be superimposed on the basic plan of a proposed manoeuvre.

The shallow water effects of interaction, and increased squat, play an important part in determining the route and time scale to be used. It will be remembered that stopping distances and turning circles increase and that pressure differences could well deflect the ship from its intended path. The researchers have described the nature of these effects and laboratory models have been used to demonstrate them individually. However, it is probable that a number of these variables will be acting at any one instant. Thus the successful conclusion of a harbour passage will remain very much dependent on the shiphandler's practical appreciation of these variable factors as it will be difficult, if not impossible, to quantify them accurately enough for safe guide lines to be laid down to cover every conceivable circumstance.

So far as the problem of squat is concerned, the situation is somewhat better in that most ports are now able to indicate the minimum acceptable underkeel clearance for normal working. Even in this situation, local conditions such as distance of travel, time available, the position of shallows and bends and traffic density, will all have to be taken into account when assessing the speed required, in relation to the time available, for the passing of specific obstacles. As the degree of squat varies with speed, this factor must be kept to the forefront when planning the transit.

It must also be remembered that although there may be similarities between open water and enclosed water shiphandling, in the former the energy generated by the ship's movement may easily be dissipated and cause little ill effect, whereas in an enclosed dock or canal this is not the case and the consequent reaction and ill effects must be anticipated and allowed for. This therefore makes control of speed and correct positioning in an enclosed waterway absolutely critical and essential to a successful entry or exit.

A further consideration when making an arrival or departure is that for most ships 'time is money'. Although a transit through the area at the slowest speed possible will minimise the adverse effects so far as your own ship and the environment is concerned, a higher speed must be chosen to take account of the commercial necessity of the port to maximise its potential capacity to move cargo and passengers between sea and hinterland while keeping its operating costs to a reasonable level.

Control of Speed Through the Water

There are three main areas of concern for the shiphandler when choosing a speed in a confined space, namely:

1. the effects on own ship;
2. the effect on other ships, both underway and moored;
3. the effect on walls, banks and installations.

Taking the effect on own ship first, it is clear that increasing the speed through the water increases the interaction forces generated. Excessive speed leads inevitably to loss of control. As the speed increases pressure builds up ahead of the hull and too much disturbance at the stern creates a breakdown of the streamlines into the rudder, leading to a loss of effectiveness. The result of persisting with too high a speed is a tendency to sheer from side to side of the waterway with the distinct possibility that such control that does remain will be lost, with a collision or grounding the likely outcome.

The effect on other ships underway may be two-fold. Firstly, the water being pushed ahead of the ship will cause the water level to rise for considerable distances ahead and this could be instrumental in causing other vessels with low overhead clearances to contact obstructions such as bridges and power lines. Secondly, the water being pushed ahead may create a slopping effect at the end of a section and adversely effect the manoeuvrability of a vessel entering a lock, or berthing.

The effect of excessive speed through the water on other ships already moored, particularly those which are improperly secured, can be quite dramatic. For example, long before the offending vessel comes into view, and therefore without warning, the water pushed ahead and the slopping effect together can cause a badly moored vessel to start ranging and, unless immediate action is taken to tighten or strengthen the moorings, cause her to break adrift. To guard against this possibility vessels moored at canal and riverside berths should ensure that their moorings are adequate in quality and number and that they are properly attended at all times. Self-tensioning winches are not at their best under these surging conditions and should not be used in this mode of operation. In the case of a ship passing a moored vessel at very high speed not even the best moorings are likely to be able to withstand the strains imposed. This is particularly true where both the moored vessel and the passing ship are at or near to the draft limits of that section.

Finally, the effect on banks, walls and installations. Some erosion is inevitable in any waterway but there can be no doubt that a vessel transitting at too high a speed will greatly accelerate the damage by the suction effect of the pressure wave following astern. The 'slopping' effect mentioned earlier can also be the cause of lock gates parting and then slamming together again with some violence.

It is impossible to be specific about what constitutes a safe speed through the water in a canal, river or dock system, since it will vary from vessel to vessel and even with the same vessel at different conditions of loading and trim. However, it is certain that if the ship is creating considerable disturbance close astern, and is requiring an excessive use of the helm to hold the desired course line within a channel, then that ship is being operated close to the limits of controllability. A reduction of propeller speed would then be prudent and possibly cost little in terms of time, and certainly would lead to a saving on the harbour authority's maintenance account.

The technique for choosing a speed should be to gradually achieve a rate through the water at which the ship is comfortable and responsive to the helm and is causing neither too much pressure ahead nor disturbance astern. The critical points are the blockage factor and the necessity to reduce or stop, intentionally or otherwise. For a ship whose blockage factor is fifty or sixty per cent this speed may be as little as two or three knots.

Stopping the Ship

To bring the vessel to a controlled stop is extremely important; to do otherwise can at best lead to acute embarrassment. In open sea but fairly shallow water, the use of steady astern power and full rudder brings a vessel to a fairly rapid stop, but the final heading is likely to have altered by about ninety degrees. If, with a similar depth to draft ratio, a stop is made with engine and rudder being used to maintain the initial heading, the stopping distance increases by perhaps twenty five per cent. In an enclosed water, the latter case is the more likely, as most river and canal passages there is little lateral room available for manoeuvring.

Stopping a ship or taking way off in relation to the control of speed, can cause concern in even the most experienced shiphandler. How adversely a vessel's manoeuvring characteristics will be affected by the shallow water commonly found in harbours, and how they will be further influenced by the interaction effects generated by the vessel's own movement through the water can never be accurately assessed. A reasonable speed through the water, for the simple purpose of making a passage, may so easily prove to be excessive, through the water, when it comes to maintaining control while 'taking it off', particularly in an emergency.

Loss of rudder effectiveness and the failure of the propeller to 'bite' when going astern are the twin problems to be coped with when 'bringing up'. Both are influenced by shallow water and also, particularly in an emergency situation, by the stern wave catching up and then overtaking the vessel. The technique for bringing the ship to a stop is, in normal circumstances, to make a gradual deceleration maintaining propeller bite and rudder effectiveness. In the emergency situation however, gradual deceleration being ruled out, propeller bite and rudder effectiveness must still be maintained so far as possible. This is best accomplished by relatively short spells of engine going astern alternated with whatever short 'kicks' of the engine ahead, with the helm hard over, that may be necessary to keep control of direction.

Choosing a Correct Position in a Channel

The importance of correct positioning in a restricting waterway, where interaction effects are likely, cannot be stressed too highly. On the one hand it is essential for safety, and on the other, it frequently permits a faster transit. What is often not appreciated about correct positioning is the effort of concentration required to maintain it over long distances or periods of time. The benefit of making sure that deck ratings keep their 'touch' with the manual steering pays under these circumstances. It is not without due cause that pilots in the Manchester Ship Canal, for example, extol the virtues of the specialist helmsman service offered to shipowners in their district.

In general the only place to be when transitting a canal or narrow river, certainly at optimum speed and for safety and comfort at all speeds, is in the middle of the channel. In this context the 'middle' means the centre of usable water, which is not necessarily the midpoint between the banks. This is the case where the banks are regular and the water depth constant between them, but not where the channel is of irregular shape with uneven banks, bends, siltings, rocky outcrops and inlets. It is important also to remember that the whole vessel should be in the centre or neutral water, because around this middle line the shiphandler can expect the pressures and interaction effects to be approximately equal, and rudder effectiveness is at its best, with more or less similar amounts of helm either side of amidships being required to maintain position. Indeed, assuming no error in the steering gear, one can be sure that the vessel is out of position, i.e. off the middle line, if consistently more helm is required to one side of amidships than the other.

The principal evil to be guarded against is *bank suction effect* which can, if not readily appreciated and allowed for, soon take over, making rudder control difficult or even impossible. *Bank rejection* is another problem if a somewhat lesser one in practice, perhaps because it is more easily perceived than bank suction. Since the magnitude of both these forms of interaction are related directly to speed through the water, it may be necessary when affected by either or both, in order to re-establish control, to effect a gradual reduction in speed while aligning the vessel in the correct position in the channel.

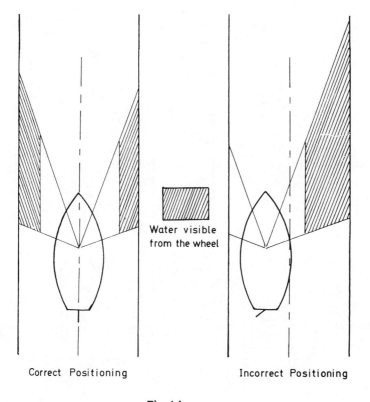

Correct Positioning   Incorrect Positioning

Fig.6.1

Positioning in a narrow channel

In Figure 6.1, the shaded areas indicate the water visible from the wheel because these areas are a useful indication to the helmsman of the vessel being in the middle and straight. However, if the size or construction of the ship is such that the helmsman can see little or no water at the edges it will then be necessary for the master or pilot to control the ship's heading by giving helm orders. This method is a tedious and relatively inefficient means of controlling progress during a long canal

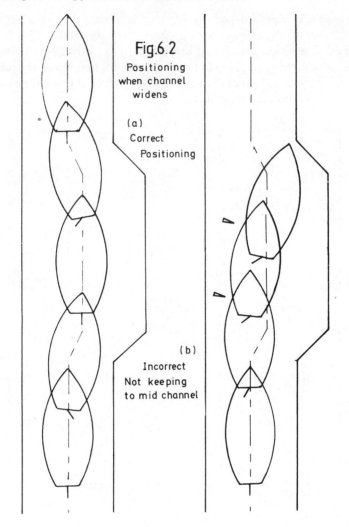

Fig.6.2
Positioning when channel widens

(a) Correct Positioning

(b) Incorrect Not keeping to mid channel

or river transit. Figure 6.2 shows correct and incorrect positioning for negotiating a widening of the waterway. The consequences of bad positioning become apparent, either in the approach, or on late reaction to the imbalance of forces on entering the wider area. Obviously corrective action should be taken to avoid ending up as illustrated in Figures 6.2 b, c and d. Where, however, the bad positioning is accompanied by excessive speed, corrective action may not be successful.

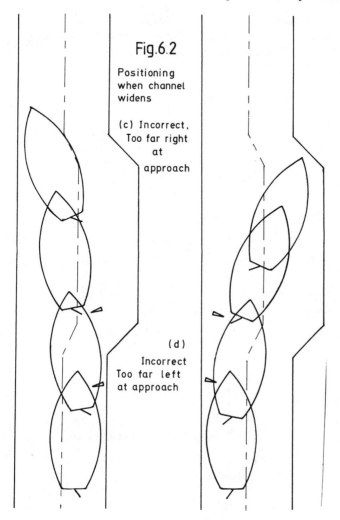

Fig.6.2

Positioning
when channel
widens

(c) Incorrect,
Too far right
at

approach

(d)

Incorrect
Too far left
at approach

Turning the Ship

As described earlier the act of turning a ship's wheel does not mean that an instantaneous alteration of course will occur but that, in due time and with sufficient space, the vessel will swing through the required arc. The larger the vessel the greater the time and space required. For a large tanker (approximately 320,000 tonnes displacement) over three minutes, from the wheel being put over, is required to swing through 43 degrees under full starboard helm made at about half speed. At the end of this time the ship will have moved a further half mile along her original course line and her after third will be to the left of the course line, the forward two thirds to the right (Fig. 6.3).

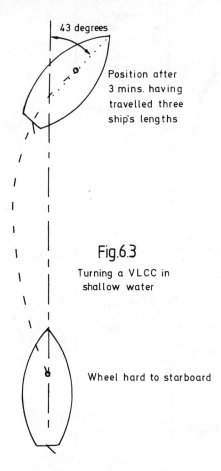

43 degrees

Position after
3 mins. having
travelled three
ship's lengths

Fig.6.3

Turning a VLCC in
shallow water

Wheel hard to starboard

This means that an alteration of course has to be anticipated by a period of several minutes in a large ship and, furthermore, it is important to remember in a collision avoidance situation that the original course and speed of the ship do not change for some considerable time, although the aspect presented to an oncoming vessel may well have changed by many degrees. A turn of over 50 degrees under full helm may have to be completed before all the vessel clears the initial course line. Large vessels under 'full away' conditions may not be able to use full rudder settings in which case additional delay will be caused.

The turn described above was made in deep water, at least four times the draft. To complete the turn to 90 degrees off the original course would take about five and a half minutes with an advance of over 1000 metres and a transfer in excess of 360 metres. In similar circumstances but now having a draft to depth ratio of 1:1.2, that is a clearance factor of about twenty per cent of the draft, the turn through a right angle would take nearly eight minutes, the advance almost 1200 metres and the transfer 555 metres. A comparison of deep, medium and shallow water turns is shown in Figure 6.4.

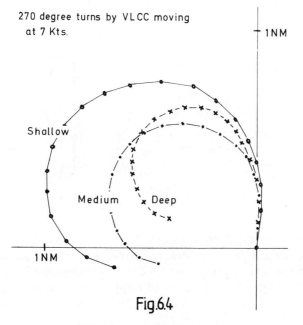

270 degree turns by VLCC moving at 7 Kts.

1NM

Shallow

Medium   x Deep

1NM

Fig.6.4

Comparison of turning circles

When turns are to be made in water restricted in width as well as depth the technique is very similar to that used for rounding a bend with a road vehicle, that is to decelerate or brake in and accelerate out, but of course adjustments cannot be made so rapidly in a ship (Fig. 6.5). With vessels whose size is small in relation to the radius of curvature of the bend, speed and positioning are less critical than with a large vessel. Points to watch out for are i) getting too close to the inside of the bend and becoming affected by bank suction, and ii) being stationed too high in the bend particularly as there is a tendency for a vessel at speed to side slip as well as turn on a bend.

With a large vessel this is relative to the radius of curvature and blockage factor. It is imperative to use the high side of the bend and

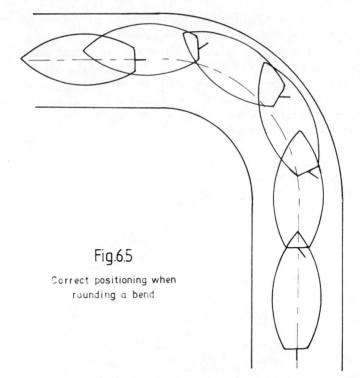

Fig.6.5

Correct positioning when
rounding a bend

ensure that speed and positioning are correct. If positioning and speed are appropriate then it is possible to balance the pressures and interaction forces so that once started round the bend the ship should require only check helm (opposite to direction of turn) to control the rate of swing as she turns.

Passing Another Vessel Underway

Meeting and passing another vessel under way in a waterway can be the most testing of shiphandling manoeuvres, particularly at night. To pass safely, whatever condition of visibility, both vessels must be handled properly, as the margins for error can be very small indeed—say 5 metres or less between ships and 6 or 7 metres between each ship and the banks or walls when they are abeam of each other. Needless to say the technique must be right, and the method employed by both vessels in concert. It would be imprudent, to say the least, to attempt to manoeuvre within such fine limits as those indicated above (and in Fig. 6.6) where there is any doubt concerning the ability of the shiphandlers involved. The proper use of VHF radio telephone and port control systems can aid the selection of time and place for critical passes.

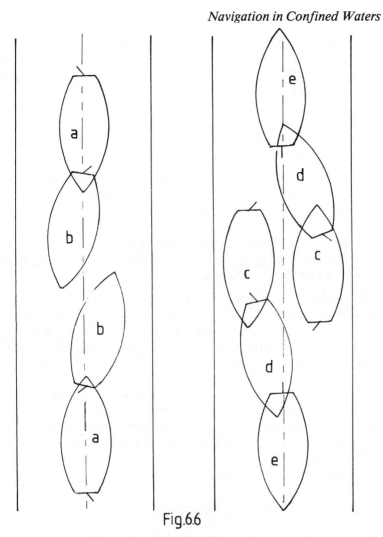

Fig.6.6

Correct positioning when passing

The standard technique is for each vessel to adjust its approach to the point of passing early enough so that, on arrival at 'a' in Figure 6.6, not only is each vessel in the position indicated (in the middle and straight) but both are proceeding at speeds through the water not greater than those considered proper for the actual passing manoeuvre. This achieves three essentials to the successful completion of the exercise; firstly the pressures ahead and disturbance close astern are minimised; secondly, from this stable position each vessel should be able to keep its engines turning ahead throughout the passing phase without materially increasing the speed through the water; and finally, the ship/ship and ship/bank interactions to be experienced when at positions 'b', 'c' and 'd' will be kept to a tolerable level.

The need to keep the engines turning throughout the passing phase must be stressed because it is fundamental to the maintenance of rudder effectiveness and it is this quality alone which will ensure that each vessel can be kept under full control and in the right position. To have to go astern on the engine at any stage can be fatal. Points requiring special attention during the passing are:

1. with the vessels at 'b' the bows will tend to reject each other;
2. when at 'c' it is too late to adjust the clearance distances, the essential thing being to maintain them as they are and keep the ships straight;
3. with the vessels at 'd' there will be a strong tendency for each to 'dive' into the space vacated by the other. This tendency usually has to be countered by a kick of full ahead and corrective helm.

Figure 6.7 shows the most common fault regarding positioning, where vessel A has attempted to pass correctly but vessel B has left the middle too soon. Once again if the speeds are reasonable the situation may be recoverable, but in extreme cases, at positions 'a' and 'b', vessel B will experience bank suction aft and will be unable to come to starboard and clear the way in time, so causing vessel A to have to reverse her propulsion at 'b' which is likely to cause her to slew across the channel and block it. Vessel B will now have to try to take way off to avoid a collision but the transverse thrust of conventional right hand propellers may not break the bank suction effect and she will continue to slew to port and perhaps into A.

Overtaking Another Vessel Underway

As with all other close quarters shiphandling manoeuvres in a narrow waterway, the technique of overtaking another vessel safely, not only reflects a proper appreciation of the pressures and interaction forces involved, but can also illustrate the best possibility of minimising their effect and overcoming them.

The most dangerous interaction to be counteracted during the manoeuvre, and one which is peculiar to it, is the ship/ship interaction when abeam of each other. This interaction tends to draw the vessels together (the reverse of the sea situation) and would, if both were proceeding at any speed through the water, lock them together. Bearing this in mind the method commonly used requires vessel A (in Fig. 6.8), which is to be overtaken, to adopt a position as far as possible over to her

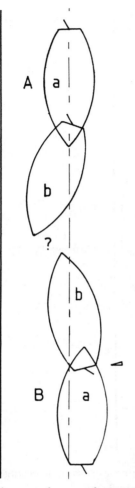

Fig. 6.7

Incorrect positioning
when passing

own bank and stopped or nearly stopped in the water. If this is done, two things are achieved, firstly any adverse influence that vessel A may exert, on the overtaking vessel B, is kept to a minimum and secondly, B ought to be able to overtake at a speed consistent with the least disturbance of A.

If B is able to follow the path indicated in Figure 6.8, i.e. the middle of the best available water, without recourse to periods of increased engine movement to maintain rudder effectiveness, then A should not be unduly disturbed. In practice, however, that situation is rarely achieved and consequently it is normal for the overtaken vessel to have to use her engines and helm to counter, firstly, a tendency for her stern to be drawn in towards the overtaking vessel as it comes on the quarter and, secondly, a tendency for the bow to follow the stern of the overtaking vessel as it moves ahead.

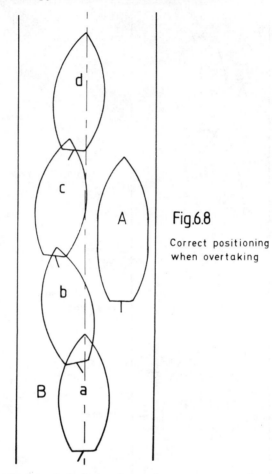

Fig.6.8

Correct positioning
when overtaking

One benefit that does derive from these two countering moves is that they tend to assist A back into the middle.

Twin Screw Ships

Many twin propeller, single rudder vessels, particularly if their blockage factor is high, have a deservedly bad reputation among canal shiphandlers. Quite apart from the considerable practical problem of keeping the propellers off the banks, in many situations it would appear that the interactions with the bank and bed affect the flow lines around the stern so that propeller and rudder effectiveness are reduced. This causes some vessels to lose the benefit of their twin screws and others to require constant variation of revolutions on each propeller to maintain directional stability.

Chapter 7
Basic Manoeuvring Situations

In any close manoeuvring situation the critical factors are the *approach angle* and *speed of approach*. The angle must be judged so that the internally and externally generated forces are either working to advantage, or if not, then neutralised if possible. Similarly the speed should be adjusted to one where the ship is always under control. Excessive speed leads to the build up of pressures around the hull and dangerous strains on cables and warps if they are being worked. Too little speed leaves the ship at the mercy of wind and tide which may not be prudent.

The following examples of simple manoeuvres are included to give the reader an idea of the principles on which he may plan his own ship's handling, or understand what others are attempting. In the figures consecutive positions of the vessel are shown in a numbered sequence. Where tidal stream, current, wind or a mean of these forces is a significant feature it is indicated by a solid arrow. The direction of the rudder is indicated by the fleche on the stern and the direction of the propeller thrust by a + sign, indicating ahead power, and − sign astern power. If the propeller is stopped or not producing thrust (neutral pitch) a 0 is used. The fractions $\frac{1}{8}$, $\frac{1}{4}$, $\frac{1}{2}$ and 1 are used to show the degree of thrust corresponding to *dead slow, slow, half* and *full speed* respectively. The actual degree to be used on a particular ship may vary from that shown, i.e. one vessel may require $+\frac{1}{2}$ whereas another will perform with similar characteristics when only $+\frac{1}{4}$ is ordered.

Unless otherwise stated, the vessel is single screw and fitted with a conventional right-handed propeller.

Turning a Ship in a Confined Space

Turning Short Round, Single Right-Handed Propeller. In conditions of light wind and the tidal stream being ahead or of no consequence, the traditional method of turning onto the reciprocal course is by using the transverse thrust of the propeller to advantage. Having crossed to the port side of the channel with due caution (see 1 in Fig. 7.1) and reduced speed to just having steerage way, the rudder should be put hard to

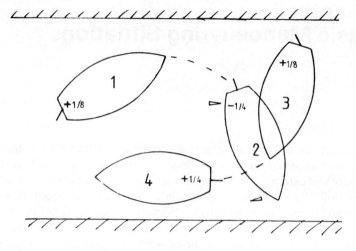

Fig.7.1

starboard with a 'kick' ahead on the engine to start the vessel swinging. As she turns across the channel, the rudder should be put amidships and propulsion reversed (2). When the ship starts to gather sternway the rudder should be put hard to starboard and the engines ahead (3). If required, movements (2) and (3) should be repeated until the turn is completed, the rudder and engines being used in each position only until way is barely made, i.e. when transverse thrust is at its maximum.

86

Turning Short Round, Single Controllable Pitch Right-Handed Propeller. In this case the propeller is continually rotating and tending to cant the stern to starboard, hence the turn is made to port. The timing of the propeller pitch and rudder movements will correspond to those in Figure 7.1. If the direction of propeller rotation is left-handed the turn will be made to starboard.

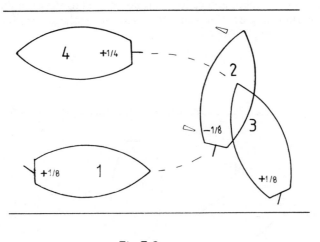

Fig.7.2

Turning Short Round, Twin Screw. Here the rudder is put hard over (Fig. 7.3) towards the chosen direction of turn and the inside propeller used to give astern power. The transverse thrust of both propellers will help to swing the ship about the required axis. If twin rudders are fitted their action becomes particularly effective.

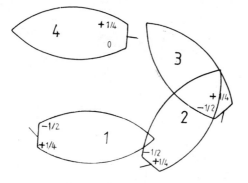

Fig.7.3

Turning Short Round, Tidal Stream or Current Astern. In this case the tidal stream or current is used (Fig. 7.4) to provide the turning force, using a single anchor which is 'snubbed' (or dredged). A slight sheer is put on the ship and the up-stream anchor let go so that the anchor and about half a shackle of cable are on the river bed. In strong flows the turn may take some distance to complete and as the ship comes to the anchor, the propellor and rudder should be used to steer the ship through the remaining angle and to stem the stream while the anchor is hove up.

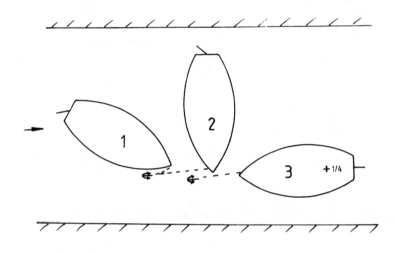

Fig.7.4

Turning the Ship Using the Bank. This method (Fig. 7.5) should not be used without first carefully checking the nature of the ground, its contours and holding characteristics. It is, however, used to good effect in several parts of the world. A sheer is put on the vessel, usually to starboard, and the bow is allowed to gently take the ground. The transverse thrust of the propeller going astern will cause the stern to swing further to port as the ship comes clear of the bank. Dense overhanging vegetation on the bank can make an excellent fender on which to perform this manoeuvre.

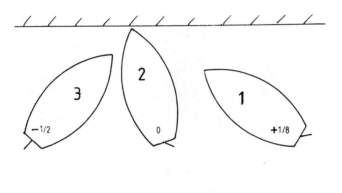

Fig.7.5

Anchoring and Mooring

Coming to a Single Anchor I. Approach the selected anchorage position from a direction about one point to starboard of dead down wind or tide (Fig. 7.6). If other ships are in the anchorage, those with similar draft and superstructure may well indicate this direction. Bring the vessel to a stop and allow her to just gather sternway before ordering 'let go the anchor'. Let the cable run out as the ship drifts astern, checking the way with the windlass or engines until the chosen number of shackles of cable are out.

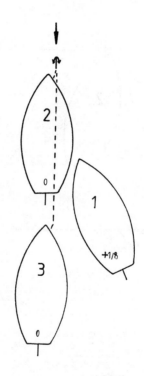

Fig.7.6

Coming to a Single Anchor II. This method (Fig. 7.7) is sometimes known as 'anchoring on the run'. At position 1 the vessel is still making a little headway as the anchor is let go. The cable runs out in a bight as the vessel swings to the tide. Care must be taken not to perform this manoeuvre at too great a speed as serious damage might be done to anchor, cable or cable handling gear plus the risk of injuring personnel.

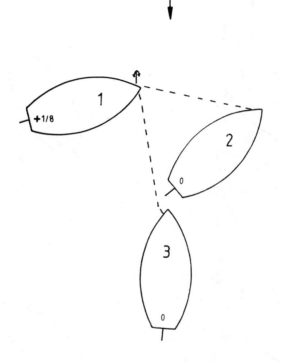

Fig.7.7

Mooring with Two Anchors—The Standing Moor. Occasionally it is necessary to use two anchors to minimise swinging arcs. The *standing moor* (Fig. 7.8) is made by letting go the up-stream anchor (at 1) and paying out the cable to twice the required length, at which time the down-stream anchor is let go (at 2). The ship is brought back to the middle position (3) by heaving on the up-stream cable and easing the down-stream.

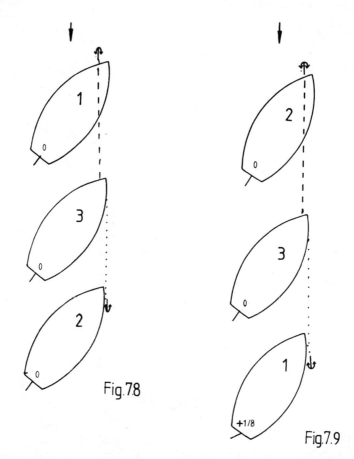

Fig. 7.8

Fig. 7.9

Mooring with Two Anchors—The Running Moor. The end result of the *running moor* is the same as the standing moor but the execution is reversed (Fig. 7.9). The down-stream anchor is let go first (at 1) and the vessel manoeuvred under power (and control) to position (2), where the second (up-stream) anchor is released. By walking back the up-stream cable and picking up the slack on the down-stream side, the middle position (3) can be attained.

Further Use of a Dredged Anchor. When there is a flow of water over the rudder the ship is capable of being steered. At anchor, in a stream, it is possible to sheer the ship on the scope of the cable (Fig. 7.10). If the cable is shortened to the point at which the anchor starts to drag it is then possible to manoeuvre the ship down stream. This technique can be used to great advantage when berthing without the assistance of tugs in strong streams.

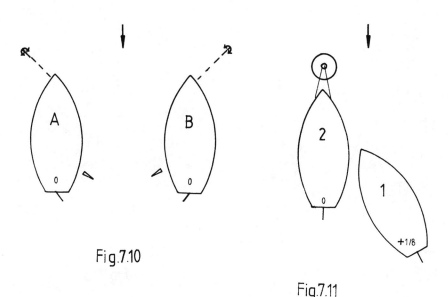

Fig.7.10

Fig.7.11

Mooring to Buoys

Securing to a Single Mooring Buoy. The buoy is approached from slightly to the right of the downwind or down tide line to allow for transverse thrust on stopping, as shown in Figure 7.11 (1). Ideally the vessel should be stopped in relation to the buoy with her bows over it enabling wires or ropes to be passed speedily (2). It must be remembered that the assistance of a mooring boat is required, and that once lines are being worked the use of the propeller would be unwise as it might bring about the release of tension in these lines causing the buoy to move rapidly endangering those working around the buoy. An astern movement would, of course, increase tension and perhaps cause ropes to part with the associated danger to those in the immediate vicinity.

In conditions of strong wind or tide the vessel should stem these forces under power.

Securing Between Two Buoys. The approach to the forward buoy is made as in Figure 7.11 and having secured to that the stern is swung to the after buoy (Fig. 7.12) and secured (2). Particular care has to be taken when the mooring boat is working near the stern.

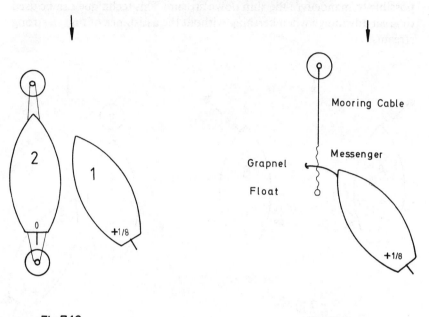

Fig.7.12   Fig.7.13

Securing to SBM's. These buoys are usually situated in open water although some may be in partially sheltered places, such as Scapa Flow in the Orkneys. The normal system of securing is to pick up a mooring rope using a grapnel to catch a floating messenger (Fig. 7.13). The messenger is brought aboard first, followed by a heavier hawser and finally chain cable. When the cable is secure the cargo pipeline is brought inboard at the bow. Numerous developments have and are being made with these systems to enable oil to be safely pumped in adverse weather conditions. Indeed, some tankers have been adapted in such a way that they can be controlled from a manoeuvring house on the forecastle during the final approach.

Berthing a Vessel

Port Side To—No Wind or Stream. The angle of approach should be quite steep—25–30 degrees (see Fig. 7.14), and the extension of the fore and aft line should meet the quay just short of the intended final position of the bow (1). The approach must be made with steerage way on until there is approximately the vessel's length left to run, at which time the rudder is put to starboard and propulsion reversed. The effect of these actions is threefold—it takes the remaining way off the vessel, introduces a degree of lateral motion and turns the vessel parallel to the quay.

The exact timing of the rudder movements and propeller reversal will vary from ship to ship, and the details given would be for a 'handy' sized motor ship. A loaded tanker with a steam turbine propulsion system would require considerably longer for the astern power to build up.

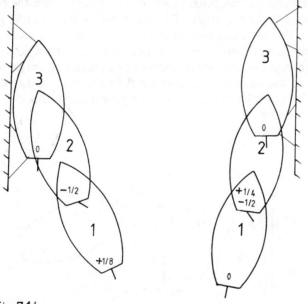

Fig.7.14

Fig.7.15

Starboard Side To—No Wind or Stream. In this instance the transverse thrust is going to act against the swing into the berth (Fig. 7.15). There-fore, the angle of approach is shallow, say 10 degrees, and head way is kept to a safe minimum. It is prudent to lead a stern rope forward to put ashore in case the stern should hang off. To induce a swing of the stern to starboard a kick of ahead power with port rudder should be given just prior to reversing propulsion and taking all way off. If the build-up of astern power is slow then a steeper approach angle should be used to allow the rudder to give a fairly high rate of turn to port and some lateral drift before the transverse thrust stops the swing. Correctly judged, the opposing forces should neutralise each other to leave the ship stopped in the water just off the berth.

Berthing Port Side To Using the Offshore Anchor—No Wind or Stream. In cases where manoeuvring room may be restricted at the berth or where it is necessary to minimise the impact on a berth, the offshore anchor can be used to gain further control over the ship (Fig. 7.16). A very steep approach is made and the anchor let go abreast of the intended final position of the bow (1) and sufficiently far off that the scope of the cable will prevent dragging. The ship is then steamed around the anchor, cable being payed out as required until just ahead of the berth and able to run a head rope (2). The propeller thrust is now reversed and the rudder put amidships as head way is lost. The ship's stern will then move in towards the berth, the bow being controlled by the head rope and cable (3).

If berthing starboard side to, the manoeuvre is carried out in a similar manner except that the turn on the anchor is taken past the point of being parallel to the quay wall to counter the transverse thrust when going astern. A stern line run at this stage, keeping the propeller clear, helps to check this swing.

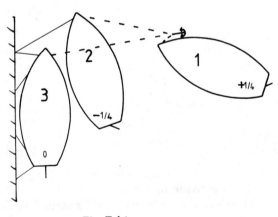

Fig.7.16

Berthing in a Tidal Stream or Current. The technique used here (Fig. 7.17) is similar to that discussed earlier when dredging the anchor. The ship must be head to the on-coming stream and the offshore anchor let go about half a ship's length ahead of the berth (1). The ship is then allowed to sheer towards the berth as the cable is payed out, rather than dredged. The reason for leaving the anchor in the stream is that it will be used for coming off the berth when the time comes. The rate of sheer can be controlled by the rudder angle, the tension in the cable, the use of the propeller and, when a head rope is being run, by using it to ease the ship alongside.

If the approach to the berth is clear then the anchor need not be used. The technique is to stem the stream, adjusting the propeller thrust to equal the effect of current or tidal stream so that the ship is stopped in relation to the ground. The rudder is then used to give lateral movement towards the berth. The rate of the stream will often slacken as the bank is approached and the propeller action should be adjusted accordingly.

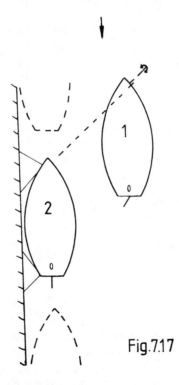

Fig.7.17

Berthing in an Offshore Wind. The effect of the wind is going to vary with the shape of the ship's superstructures, but generally the problem is to put the vessel alongside for sufficient time to run two lines ashore at each end. The approach must be positive, at a steeper angle than in calm conditions (Fig. 7.18) and aimed further aft on the berth (1). The bow should be held up to the wind by using port rudder. It will fall off rapidly under the dual effects of wind and transverse thrust so a head rope should be run and used to check the swing as the remaining way is taken off (2). This rope must be used first to check the swing and is then carried up the quay—better still two ropes may be used. On no account should weight come on a head rope as it draws aft as it will then act as a spring, causing the stern to fall off. Stern ropes must be run as soon as it is clear to do so and this is another situation where a rope might usefully be sent from well forward if no mooring boat is available.

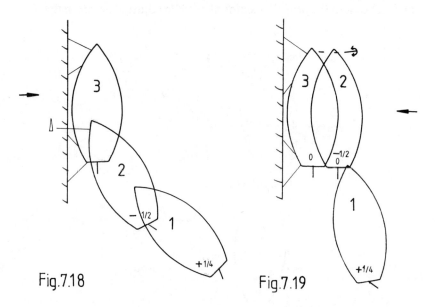

Fig.7.18   Fig.7.19

Berthing in an Onshore Wind. It is essential in these circumstances to avoid either being blown onto the quay prematurely or landing too heavily (see Fig. 7.19). Make the approach as for calm weather (1) but aim for a position several metres to weather of the berth (2). The leeway will then bring the ship alongside (3). The offshore anchor can be used to slow the rate of drift of the bow and the propeller and rudder used against a forward backspring to prevent the stern landing heavily.

98

Berthing with the Wind Ahead. The situation to be avoided here is for the wind to get inside the on-shore bow. Otherwise the braking action of the wind is an advantage (see Fig. 7.20). The approach must be more positive than in calm conditions and the astern movement judged with care to prevent the bow from swinging off. The head rope being run early will help to check this tendency.

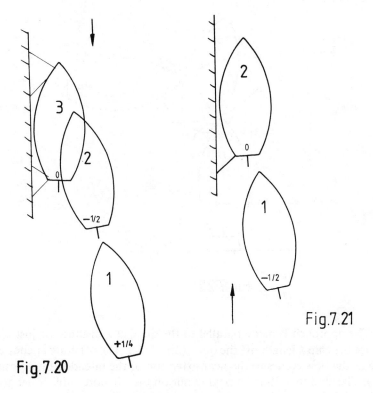

Fig. 7.20

Fig. 7.21

Berthing with the Wind Astern. This should not be attempted unless absolutely necessary as one's means of escape are limited, particularly if there is no room ahead. The danger is that a strong wind may start to push the stern away from the approach line. The approach angle should be with the wind right aft or on the offshore quarter. Astern power will be needed early as the leeway will have to be countered. A stern rope should be run at the first safe opportunity to check any swing away from the quay, but it must not be hove tight as the stern may land heavily. Sending a for'd spring will counter this last tendency. (Fig. 7.21.)

Berthing Stern to Quay (Mediterranean Moor). This method is used throughout the Mediterranean area, particularly for small craft. It is well suited to the relatively tideless conditions found in that part of the world, and promotes a high ratio of craft to quay space. Modern cargo handling systems have caused its demise in many places for loading or discharging but repair yards in several parts of the world still use this type of moor in layby berths.

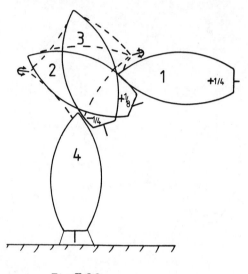

Fig.7.22

The approach is made parallel to the quay at a distance of just under twice the ship's length off the quay (Fig. 7.22). The offshore anchor is let go as the bow comes to the near extension of the intended final position (1). The ship then runs on paying out on the offshore cable to let go the second anchor on the opposite extension (2). Turning to position (3) is achieved by holding onto the offshore cable and steaming around this anchor while the cable on the shore-side anchor is kept completely slack. As the attitude approaches the right angle with the quay the propeller thrust is reversed to cause the ship to move astern towards the berth. Any tendency of the bow to swing under the transverse thrust will be damped by the anchors. Stern ropes are run to the quay and the position adjusted by use of the cables and ropes (4).

Some offshore tanker berths use a similar system but with a pattern of buoys aft instead of a quay. If some of these buoys are wide on the quarters it allows berthing to continue in conditions of wind and tide which would normally make this method unacceptable.

The Baltic Moor. This is a little used method which can be utilised on a berth which is not strong enough to bear the ship's weight. A suitable wire is secured to the anchor shackle enabling the attitude of the stern to be controlled by adjusting the tension in the wire as the vessel is turned around the anchor (Fig. 7.23). When parallel with the berth the vessel is allowed to drift towards it as cable and wire are eased. Mooring lines are run and the position adjusted as required.

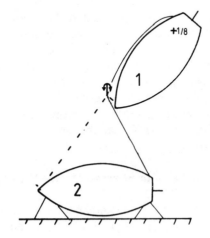

Fig.7.23

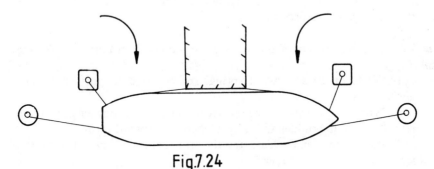

Fig.7.24

Berthing at Dolphins and Jetties. A typical tanker berth may well have a small frontage which has, therefore, to bear a disproportionate load when compared with a quay wall. The problems arising from this arrangement are that the impact on berthing must be kept as low as possible and that tidal sets and eddy currents will act on the hull in unpredictable ways even when alongside. These effects are due to the flow of water around the dolphins and jetty piers (Fig. 7.24).

On approaching or leaving the berth care has to be taken not to let the ship's extremities inside the line of the jetty head and dolphins, as this is a potentially dangerous situation which may lead to structural damage to ship and installations with their associated environmental hazards.

Leaving Berths and Moorings

When getting underway it is important to take note of the prevailing circumstances and the forces available for the shiphandler's use. These will include not only those ship borne forces mentioned many times above but additionally, levers and directly applied forces brought to bear through proper handling of ropes and cables. The principal objective is to manoeuvre the ship clear of the berth to a position where she can safely lie during the time required for the propeller to bite and the rudder to become effective. It is vital that the ship does not become out of control during this time.

Leaving a Berth—No Wind or Stream—Having been Starboard Side To (Fig. 7.25).
1. Single up to a forward spring and an after breast rope; rudder hard to starboard; slacken the breast rope; dead slow ahead.
2. Having brought the stern off the quay, put the rudder amidships; stop the propeller thrust and reverse it; let go the forward spring.
3. Allow the ship to swing parallel to the berth; stop the propeller thrust; let go aft; proceed ahead.

Leaving a Berth—No Wind or Stream—Having been Port Side To (Fig. 7.26).
1. Single up to a forward spring, rudder hard to port; dead slow ahead.
2. When the stern has swung clear, stop the propeller thrust and reverse it; put the rudder amidships; let go the forward spring.
3. As the bow comes clear, stop the propeller thrust, put the rudder to starboard and proceed ahead.

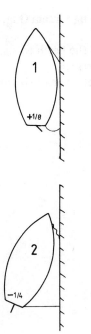

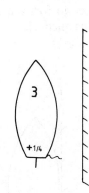

Fig.7.25

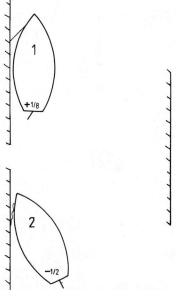

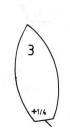

Fig.7.26

Leaving a Berth with an Oncoming Stream (Fig. 7.27).

1. Single up to a head line.

2. Put the rudder away from the berth to sheer off; use the anchor to haul off if this was laid out on arrival.

3. Let go forward and proceed ahead (if the anchor was used, after weighing anchor).

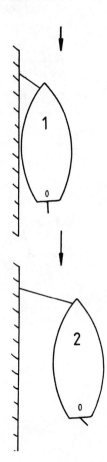

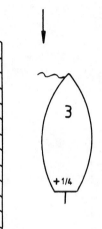

Fig.7.27

Leaving a Berth with the Stream Aft (Fig. 7.28).

1. Single up to a forward spring and a breast rope aft.

2. Ease the breast rope and allow the stream to lift the vessel off the berth. Astern propulsion might be used to lessen the strain on the for'd spring. The rudder can be used to give extra lift off the berth if necessary.

3. When the stern is clear let go aft. The propeller thrust is set to half astern to pull clear. When the weight is off the for'd spring let it go. When completely clear of the berth use appropriate rudder and proceed ahead.

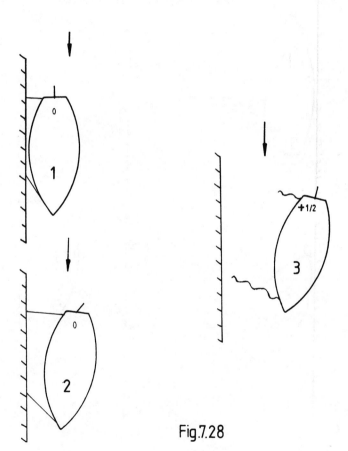

Fig. 7.28

Leaving a Berth with an Onshore Wind (Fig. 7.29).

1. Single up to a heavy forward spring led around the bow; use ahead propulsion assisted by the rudder toward the quay; swing the stern off the quay.

2. When the stern is well off the quay reverse the propulsion thrust and put the rudder amidships to clear the berth.

3. As the weight comes off the spring let it go; when the vessel is well clear of the berth put the propeller thrust in the ahead direction and use appropriate rudder to straighten the heading and proceed.

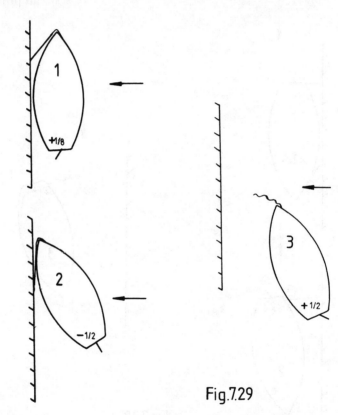

Fig. 7.29

Leaving a Berth with an Offshore Wind (Fig. 7.30).

1. Single up to a breast rope at each end and ease these to clear the berth taking care to keep the vessel aligned.

2. When clear, let go fore and aft; as the propeller comes clear of ropes in the water, proceed ahead.

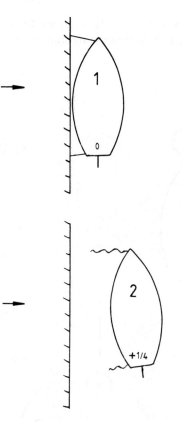

Fig.7.30

Leaving a Buoy Mooring (Fig. 7.31).

1. Single up to slip wires at each end; let go aft.

2. When clear aft use the rudder in any stream to sheer the vessel clear of the berth; if necessary a kick of the propeller might be used.

3. When clear of the forward buoy let go and proceed when the wire is clear.

If the wind or stream is aft then let go forward first. Make sure all mooring boats are clear before easing ship wires.

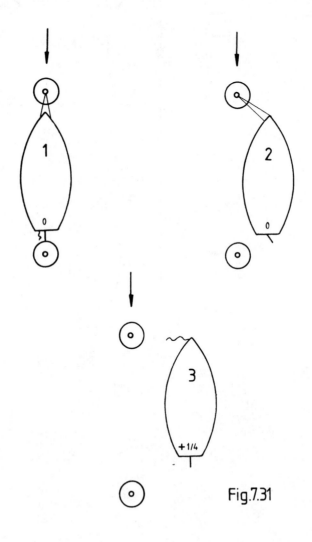

Fig.7.31

Miscellaneous Cases

Berthing a Twin Screw Ship. Using the action of the two propellers enables the ship to control her approach when berthing either side to. By adjusting the propeller revolutions, braking and turning can be achieved together; this is particularly so if twin rudders are fitted. Thus the approach should be made so that a head line can be put ashore (Fig. 7.32) and then the stern swung in towards the quay under control. In onshore or head winds, or oncoming streams, the offshore anchor may be used to steady the bow.

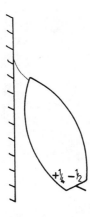

Fig.7.32

Manoeuvring a Vessel Equipped with Twin Screw, Twin Rudder and Bow Thruster. Vessels so equipped are highly manoeuvrable and can be made to move sideways enabling very fine clearances to be made. The diagram (Fig. 7.33) illustrates the procedure for leaving a berth.

1. Single up to a forward spring; put the rudders towards the quay; set the outboard propeller to give ahead propulsion (which is ducted to the quay by the rudders); balance any ahead movement by setting the inboard propeller to give astern power.

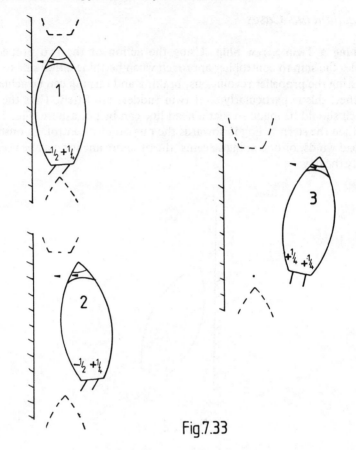

Fig.7.33

2. When the propeller thrusts are in balance let go the forward spring and use the bow thruster to ease the bow off the quay.

3. When clear of the berth the propellers can both be used to give ahead power and the rudders put amidships. The bow thruster will continue to turn the vessel to the required heading until the propellers begin to provide forward motion at which time the rudders become effective and the thruster less efficient.

Entering a Dock with Strong Flow Across the Entrance. In those ports of the world situated on river estuaries having a large rise and fall of tide (and hence strong tidal stream), enclosed docks are often used to provide constant level berths. These docks are entered through a lock, off which the stream may flow at several knots with well developed eddies and consequent silting. It can therefore be appreciated that making an entry (or exit) at some states of the tide may be hazardous and requires special techniques.

Typically, the vessel will be put alongside, stemming the tide (Fig. 7.34) at a lay-by berth just outside the lock entrance (1). Using the propeller and rudder to assist, the ship is then warped into the lock-pit using two ropes at each end, stepping one over the other to positions 2 and 3. By using such a system the ship avoids a situation where she is trying to enter at slow speed with the risk of the stern being carried with the stream, after the bow has entered still water, and as a consequence being in heavy contact with the downstream knuckle.

Leaving a lock-pit is usually easier so long as it is possible to gain sufficient way to steer safely through any eddies or rips. However, there are many places where entry and exit are restricted to certain tide related times. It is also usual in modern lock designs to include features in the plan which will minimise the risks associated with the approach, for example by angling the lock-pit or building breakwaters.

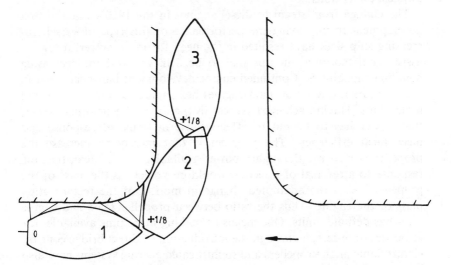

Fig.7.34

Chapter 8
Working with Tugs

Tug Design

As with most vessels, tug design is a compromise. In this case the compromise involves maximising propulsive power, manoeuvrability and safety but, at the same time, maintaining commercial viability. To increase the power available requires a larger engine and hence a bigger and less manoeuvrable hull to support the additional weight and hold its physical dimensions.

The change from steam to diesel engines in the 1950's was the first development in improving the performance of this type of vessel. Increasing ship sizes have resulted in the need for more powerful tugs to assist them mooring but this had to be achieved without decreasing handling capabilities. Continued engine development has meant that in twenty years the BHP of main engines has tripled for the same overall dimensions. Having achieved success in the area of generating power, that power has to be put to effective use in terms of response and mechanical efficiency. The problem is that merely to increase the propeller size to use the higher power available, would mean that the response to a reversal of direction would be slower, as the mass of the propeller resists the attempted change in motion of the reciprocating mass of the engine. Thus the ratio between propeller mass and engine mass has definite limits. One means of making more time available, for responses to orders, is through the introduction of direct bridge control. Controllable pitch propellers and sophisticated gearing systems have also increased flexibility.

The usual measure of a tug's performance is its bollard pull. Further comparison of efficiency can be made by the ratio of bollard pull to BHP. When shrouded, propellers can be smaller and the bollard pull to BHP ratio is improved by about twenty per cent, though efficiency when not towing is decreased.

The development of new types of propulsive systems, such as Voith Schnieder and Schottle, has also meant that manoeuvring ability has vastly improved by comparison with the open propeller, single rudder tugs. Those systems, where the thrust has directional properties, also

112

improve tugs' safety as they enable thrust to be used effectively to counter any forces which act to move the vessel sideways causing a capsizing moment or girting.

The safety of tugs has often been a cause for concern as there have been many losses due to swamping, girting and being run down. Swamping can occur relatively easily due to the low freeboard. If caught by unexpected seas with weather deck hatches open, particularly engine room skylights, a vessel may not recover. Being girted is a form of broaching and again the hull is capsized and overwhelmed by water coming through deck openings. The remedy to these two problems perhaps lies in increasing the watertight integrity of hulls and moving all accommodation above the main deck to enable easier escape and discourage the temptation to leave hatches open. Running down, however, will always be a risk when ships are operating in close company. Constant awareness of this risk in both vessels involved, and the improved manoeuvring characteristics of tugs which may aid escape from a potentially dangerous situation, are the best means of averting this kind of accident.

Tugs have developed in many ways other than being simply a towing vessel. Many have ancillary capabilities as fire-fighting and anti-pollution vessels in addition to their role as harbour tugs, ocean going tugs, or tractor type working with large trains. Other designs double as supply vessels for use in the offshore oil industry.

Deep Sea Towing

The principal shiphandling situation, when taking a tow at sea, is the manoeuvring during the time the tow line is being passed and secured. The techniques of seamanship used in securing the tow, and the specification of the towing hawser used in this operation, are not the concern of this section and are well documented elsewhere. However, the relationship between the two ships concerned and the conduct of the tow are very real shiphandling problems.

Passing the tow line in calm conditions presents relatively few problems, as the tug will not suffer any loss of manoeuvrability due to the sea state. From a position close by, or even alongside, the tow line may be passed and secured before being taken up. As the weather freshens, the rates of drift and attitudes of the two vessels in the prevailing sea will differ and the tug will suffer loss of efficiency due to the broken streamlines around its hull. In these circumstances the tug master must carefully assess the respective performances before taking his vessel into a position from which a line can be passed, and from which he can safely send away a messenger followed by a tow line. In some circumstances it may be beneficial to tow stern first but, whichever method is chosen, the tug must avoid colliding with his charge during this part of the operation and remain in a position from which the tow can be taken up easily when all is secure.

The critical part of the task is to start the tow moving without breaking or straining any gear. Way should be gathered slowly and revolutions should not be increased until the tow is moving. This may be done by either taking up station ahead or up to 90 degrees off the tow's fore and aft line. In the latter case the tow line can be brought under tension, inducing some turning moment in the tow, before being lead ahead and headway made, perhaps lessening the chances of snatching.

Once underway the provisions of the Regulations for Preventing Collisions at Sea must be adhered to. The 1972 Regulations give a great deal of privilege to towing vessels restricted in their ability to manoeuvre, but this does not mean that the responsibilities upon the towing vessel can be avoided. Should it be necessary to alter course for any reason great care should be taken and, so far as possible, the alteration should be made in steps to allow the tow to settle on each heading and avoid violent yawing and sheering. Yawing will cause unnecessary strain on the gear and should be minimised by steering the tow if manned and capable. Otherwise, trimming the towed vessel by the stern or streaming a drogue from her right aft, will improve the stability of the tow. Difficult ocean tows often require a second tug to be secured aft of the tow to provide a steadying force.

Use of Tugs in Harbours, Rivers and Canals

The role of the tug in restricted waters changes from the towing role used for mainly 'dead' tows in open water to being a manoeuvring aid to a larger ship. This assistance may be to help provide directional stability at low speeds or in tight bends and to act as a thruster when coming on or off a berth. Practices vary throughout the world with the European nations generally using their tugs fore and aft on short wires or bridles, whereas the American technique frequently requires the tugs to act as thrusters free to move to the position of greatest advantage. In general, their use makes little difference to the practice of the basic manoeuvring principles discussed in Chapter 7, but they undoubtedly assist in the control of speed and the maintenance of correct position. The following examples illustrate some of the ways in which tugs can be used to aid the locking and berthing of ships.

Entering a Lock I. In Fig. 8.1 a conventionally powered ship in loaded condition is approaching a lock preparatory to entering a dock system. A tug is secured at each end prior to lining the vessel up for the approach and a third is in attendance to act as thruster to counter the tidal eddy off the lock entrance. The vessel should be lined up with the lock, allowing sufficient distance off to make any necessary corrective ahead movements, and a course held at sufficient speed to maintain steerage way in order to bring up in the lock reasonably close and parallel to the appropriate side. As the ratio of lock length and breadth to the ship's dimensions is assumed to be of the order of two to one there is sufficient room to use port helm, if desired, to counteract the cant of an astern movement. The task of the head and stern tugs is to assist in maintaining the right heading, and as there is sufficient room in the lock they can both be kept secured throughout.

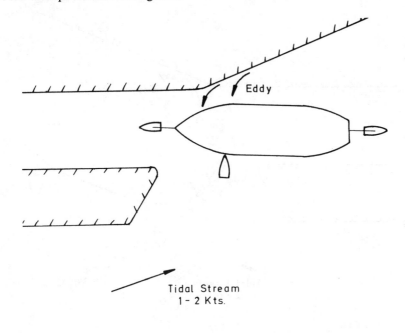

Eddy

Tidal Stream
1 - 2 Kts.

Fig. 8.1

The control of the tugs is often by use of whistle signals although the increasing use of VHF radio telephone has, in many instances, superceded the former method.

Entering a Lock II. In fresher conditions with stronger tidal streams and an onshore wind, the technique is varied to use these forces to the

115

greatest advantage (Fig. 8.2). The vessel is angled in a position close up to the entrance so that she is making leeway across the line of the lock. The rate of making leeway is controlled by the tugs and the cushioning effect of the tidal eddy; forward motion at this juncture, is minimal. When the approach line starts to open the stern tug is sent round to the trail position. As this manoeuvre by the tug has to be done on a tight wire it will tend to lift the stern and cause the bow to fall off to starboard and this should be anticipated and countered. The tug on the port shoulder is used to hold the bow up to the wind and counteract any rejection sheer caused as the stern clears the knuckle on the pierhead. The port tug must now be slipped and the propeller used to give sufficient speed for the rudder to be effective. This action might make the approach speed higher than would be used in calmer conditions and this way must be checked by the stern tug once in the lock.

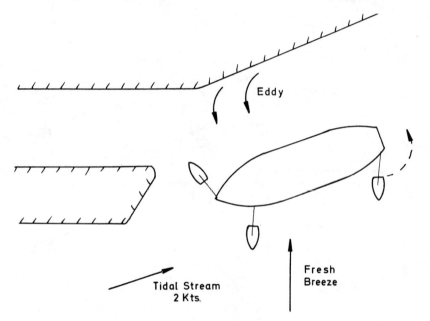

Eddy

Fresh
Breeze

Tidal Stream
2 Kts.

Fig. 8.2

The above illustrations are examples of well tried methods but, with the advent of larger ships and manoeuvring systems, variations have to be made. Consider the case of a twin screw turbine powered container ship whose length and breadth are about three quarters those of the lock-pit—no bow thruster fitted. The head tugs would be positioned as in Figure 8.1 and two stern tugs in the trail position used to give stopping power because of the slow reaction of the turbines. The vessel would be brought up outside the lock, aligned with the lock axis and taken in slowly. In fresh conditions, as in Figure 8.2, because of her size and freeboard a direct approach cannot be made and the best method would be to ease the ship onto the fendered wall before warping into the lock.

On the other hand, a ship of the same size as that discussed in Figures 8.1 and 8.2 but equipped with twin controllable pitch propellers and a powerful bow thruster, may, in reasonable conditions of tidal stream and weather, enter the lock without the assistance of tugs as her forward speed is capable of accurate adjustment and astern power is immediately available. The thruster will aid directional stability and the propellers, used in opposition, can induce transverse motion aft, without increasing headway.

These examples have shown the tugs being used to counter tidal streams and wind from one direction. However, it can be appreciated that the use of tugs is flexible and may be adapted to counter external forces. Consider the following example of a single screw motor ship with a beam about three quarters of the lock width:

Entering a Lock III. From a position stemming the tide the vessel is brought into a position almost abeam of the entrance, out of the strongest flow of the stream but with room to swing to port (Fig. 8.3).

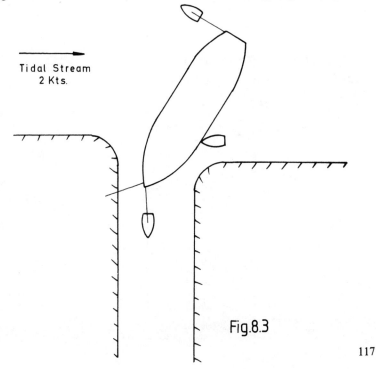

Tidal Stream
2 Kts.

Fig.8.3

Using the minimum of forward motion she is swung to port by the head tug and the downstream drift is checked by the tug positioned on the port side near the pivoting point. When the bow is close to the upstream knuckle a head rope is sent away, hove tight and secured. When this rope is fast, the stern tug can lift the stern to align the vessel with the lock and as she does so the head rope can be moved along the lock and the vessel steamed slowly in.

Berthing a VLCC. The movement should be timed, if necessary, to coincide with slack water or the first of the ebb (if mooring 'bows in'). Way is taken off slowly but steerage control maintained as long as possible. The tugs are secured, bows to the ship, in order to act as thrusters at each end. The action of the tugs becomes more efficient as the headway is reduced. The tanker is brought up off the berth and eased alongside slowly, parallel to the jetty head (Fig. 8.4). It must be remembered that the great mass of such a ship will meet the berth with considerable force unless the rate of approach is extremely slow, and also because of her length in proportion to the length of the jetty is great, it will not be easy to ascertain whether or not the ship is parallel to the berth. In both instances instruments can be of great help to give the distance off and the rate of approach and also the heading and rate of turn.

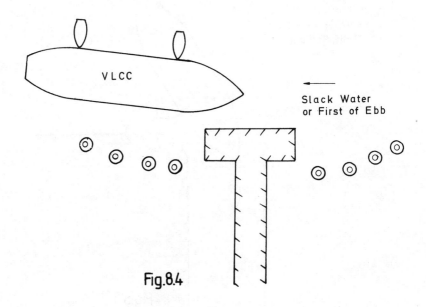

Fig.8.4

Interaction Between Tug and Ship

A relatively small vessel like a tug, operating in the vicinity of much larger vessels, will experience the results of *interaction forces* and in certain circumstances these can lead to dangerous situations. It has been shown earlier that when two ships are steaming side by side, pressure builds up as the flow lines become restricted by their hull forms, tending to push their bows apart. Similarly, with a tug and ship this reaction will occur but because of the difference in masses the effect on the tug will be more apparent. Also in the beam to beam situation there is a force acting to pull the ships together which will succeed if it becomes greater than the hull's resistance to lateral motion.

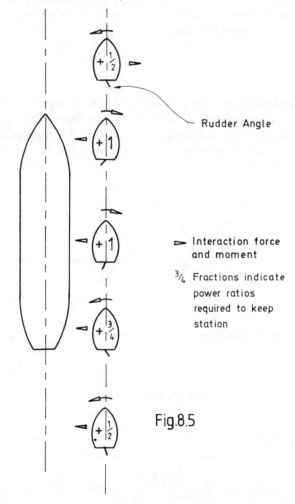

Rudder Angle

◻ Interaction force and moment

$^3/_4$ Fractions indicate power ratios required to keep station

Fig.8.5

The turning effects must be countered by the tug's rudder and the attraction (or repulsion) by increasing the speed to improve the directional stability. Situations may therefore occur where, due to excessive speed by the ship or mishandling by the tugmaster, the interaction forces become too great for the tug to counter and a serious accident may occur. Such an incident could either result in the lack of manoeuvrability of the tug, effectively immobilising it as an aid to the larger vessel, or, more seriously, could lead to the tug being trapped under the bows of an oncoming ship and being run down. Figure 8.5 illustrates the variation of these forces for differing stations taken by the tug. Having studied the figure it can be appreciated why modern propulsion systems using vectored thrust are becoming increasingly popular with tug crews as they are then able to apply the tug's own forces in direct opposition to those which might draw them into danger.

Girting

Should a tug find herself being towed by the vessel she is supposed to be assisting, it can happen that the forces acting on the tug through the towline are greater than her self-generated forces. If this force is acting in a direction at or near the perpendicular to the tug's fore and aft line it may lead to the nearside gunwhales of the tug being towed under (Fig. 8.6)

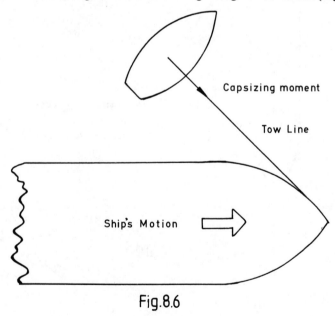

Capsizing moment

Tow Line

Ship's Motion

Fig.8.6

Girting a Tug

and if either the line cannot be released or hatches have been left open, then the tug might well be capsized. This is another circumstance in which vectored thrust is at an advantage over conventional propulsion.

If the tug cannot steam out of the situation, there may be the possibility of shipping the tow from the tug or perhaps to severing the tow line aboard the ship.

Chapter 9
Pilots, Pilotage Waters and Bridge Procedures

The Master/Pilot Relationship

The relationship between a ship's pilot and her master is a unique one, and one which in the English legal system has established a considerable case law. It is not the purpose of this book to delve deeply into the legal position of the parties, but by the nature of the subject it can never be far from the surface. The reason for this is easy to see because in almost all ports, rivers and canals of the world the master retains responsibility for his ship although the pilot is, for all practical purposes, the person in operational control during the transit. The precedents in English Law are reasonably clear as to the theoretical relationship between master and pilot, but the actual relationship on the bridge, in real time and under the various pressures, physical and psychological, of current marine commercial practice, make this boundary a little more vague.

It is apparent that the master is the person in charge from the point of view that he, and he alone, has command of the ship. He is responsible for the discipline of her crew, which includes the obedience to lawful commands and also the duties contained in the Regulations for Preventing Collisions at Sea requiring the posting of lookouts and the provision of proper lights and shapes. The pilot, on the other hand, normally has charge of the 'conduct' of the vessel and will be responsible for decisions such as whether or not to proceed, when and where to anchor and what course and speed the vessel should make while in the district.

Difficulty arises when the master decides that the pilot is not conducting the vessel in a proper manner. The case law indicates that the master has no right to interfere with the pilot except in cases of the pilot's intoxication or manifest incapability, or in cases in which the pilot does not foresee danger, or in other cases of great necessity. This would at first sight appear to be a fairly clear decision but when examined in the practical sense it presents problems. For example, at what point in time does a person become intoxicated? Similarly, how is the master to judge between a difficult situation which may arise partially as a result of the pilot's negligence but which is not beyond the 'point of no return', and circumstances where the safety of the vessel can only be restored by the action of the master using skill and knowledge superior to that of the pilot? In the former example it is hardly possible to ask the pilot for a breath, blood or urine sample and make an objective decision of his probable lack of efficiency, and in the latter case the pilot's defence that he had to take a certain course of action because of his local knowledge is often difficult to refute.

In either case the master faces a decision which may have serious repercussions, as he will have to justify any action of relieving the pilot, to his owners if there is an accident or delay, and perhaps to an enquiry in the port concerned. The pressure therefore acts to cause the master to delay taking any steps to relieve the pilot, unless the evidence is overwhelming as to his incompetence or incapacity.

A pilot boarding a ship which in his opinion is unseaworthy, through the incompetence or incapability of the master or crew, is in a difficult situation, and it is a point on which there is little case law in the United Kingdom. Had the unseaworthiness been due to a mechanical failure then it is a fairly clear question of fact on which the local regulations probably back the pilot by stating that a vessel may not enter the district unless she is in a fit condition. The difficulty facing a pilot in exercising his judgement in the former case probably arises from the nature of his contract which is usually one of self-employment. Thus if he declines his 'turn' because of an opinion rather than a clear fact it is likely that another pilot may offer his services. Alternatively, the problem may not become apparent until the transit is partially complete, leading to a situation where self-interest dictates that one makes the best of a bad job.

Thankfully, the great majority of transits through pilotage waters pass without serious incident, but it is important that each party is aware of the legal position of the other and there can be little doubt that in most situations a great weight lies on the master with whom the liability invariably stops.

Taking a Pilot Aboard

It is the clear responsibility of the master of a ship to see that a pilot who is expected to board has safe means of doing so. In harbour the means of boarding is usually the gangway or accommodation ladder which must provide safe access. When at sea, unless the freeboard is very low the boarding is by:

1. pilot ladder.
2. pilot ladder and accommodation ladder (when the freeboard is greater than 9 metres).
3. pilot hoist.
4. helicopter.

Regulation for all these methods is by internationally agreed conventions and instructions which, in the first three cases, are laid down in British Law by the Merchant Shipping (Pilot Ladder) Rules 1965, (S.1. 1965 No. 1046) as amended by the Merchant Shipping (Pilot Ladders) (Amendment No. 2) Rules 1972, (S.1. 1972 No. 531). In the case of helicopters being used the guidance given by the International Chamber of Shipping should be referred to.

The Pilot Ladder Rules state which classes of vessel are obliged to carry pilot ladders and contain strict rules as to their size, fitting, construction and use. They also state that their rigging must be properly supervised and that the ladder and its access must be adequately illuminated.

Pilot hoists are the subject of similar rules regarding their construction and use. One of the principal rules is that a standard pilot ladder must be rigged, ready for use, in addition to a mechanical hoist. The reason for this is that pilot hoists have proved to be unsafe in certain circumstances and are viewed with suspicion by many pilots and pilotage authorities.

From the shiphandling point of view it is the duty of the master to provide safe conditions for the pilot boat to approach the ship's side and remain there while the pilot and his effects are brought safely aboard the vessel. It is the normal practice to discuss the details of this transfer by radio telephone as the ship approaches the pilot station. The pilot vessel will manoeuvre to launch her sea-boat safely and instruct the waiting ship which side the pilot ladder should be rigged, adding any further information which may be relevant, such as the ideal height of the foot above the water line. The receiving ship should then be turned to create a lee on the boarding side. So long as sea room and other shipping allow this is a relatively easy task in sheltered waters as the ship's hull will protect the pilot launch from wind and small wind waves. When a swell is running there is little that the ship can do but try to hold a heading on which rolling is minimised, without going too fast for the launch to be able to manoeuvre safely. It is usual for the propeller(s) to be stopped during the time taken for boarding to avoid unnecessary injury should anyone fall into the sea.

In conditions where fresh wind is causing large sea waves, it is possible to use the ship's wake in a tight turn to flatten the sea sufficiently for the launch to make her approach and for the pilot to reach the relative safety of the ladder, before the vessel steadies on a new heading (Fig. 9.1).

Disembarking a Pilot

This operation can be divided into three distinct phases, when out bound:

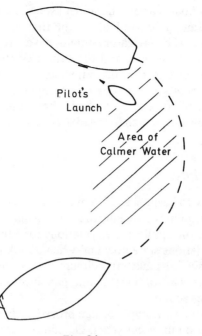

Fig.9.1

Making.a lee for a Pilot Boat

1. the approach to the pilot station;
2. disembarking the pilot;
3. clearing the pilot station.

When inbound the pilot can usually go ashore in the conventional way. Should there be a change of pilot it is customary for the new pilot to relieve the old on the bridge before taking his leave, and as this will be a feature of that pilotage it is usually done with little fuss.

When approaching the pilot station outbound, the master will be advised by the departing pilot as to the details of positioning the ladder, the approach to the pilot station and any local features relevant to the ship's departure. The pilot will then leave the bridge to go down to his disembarkation position leaving the master to make the final approach.

The disembarkation is performed under constraints similar to those when the pilot boards at sea, with respect to making a lee for the launch to come alongside. The rigging of the ladder and disembarkation must be supervised by a responsible officer and again it is usual to stop the propeller during the time the pilot is over the ship's side and boarding his boat.

125

Once the pilot boat is away, the ship must be conned safely clear of the pilotage station and a course laid for the first stage of the voyage to a new destination. The navigator should have prepared the necessary information prior to sailing, and the officer of the watch should now advise the master of this information, which is a change from his role of monitoring the pilot's navigational performance. When settled on her course and clear of congestion at the harbour entrance, the master will normally hand over the watch to the officer on bridge duty.

Bridge Procedures

The IMCO guide to keeping a safe navigational watch defines the watch-keeper's responsibilities as being the safe navigation of the vessel and compliance with the applicable Regulations for Preventing Collisions at Sea. These regulations state how and when a lookout must be kept, the speed a vessel should make, the circumstances where one vessel must keep out of the way of others and guidance as to the timing and magnitude of this action.

The organisation of a ship's bridge procedure has been the subject of much consideration in recent years. Guidance is contained in the *Bridge Procedures Guide* published by the International Chamber of Shipping. This is further amplified by 'M' notice number 854 entitled *Navigation Safety* which draws attention to the fact that the majority of marine accidents are due to human error. Many of these mishaps are caused by relevant navigational information either not being available or if available not reaching the person in charge of the bridge.

The use of ship's bridge simulators to improve the training of personnel in collision avoidance, pilotage, manoeuvring and berthing is a valuable method of developing standard procedures and team effort. The collection of navigational data, collating it by priority and presenting this information to the master, pilot or officer of the watch, is an area of increasing research throughout the world. Shiphandling can only be improved when the person making decisions concerning a ship's behaviour is fully aware of *all* the facts relating to a planned manoeuvre and has the means at his disposal to achieve his objective with the optimum use of available resources.

Chapter 10
The Management of Passages and Manoeuvres

The natural shiphandler is blessed with the ability to make his ship do exactly what he wants when he wants. Such gifts are endowed upon very few of us, and we have to resort to a more scientific approach to the art. In the earlier chapters some of the forces acting on a ship in various conditions of sea, weather, draft and propulsion were discussed. With this knowledge of the effects of self and externally applied forces to the ship's hull it is now possible to begin the operation of handling the ship.

Planning

Any operation should be carefully planned before attempting its execution. The experienced ship's pilot may well do this task in his head but for difficult harbour movements the pilot, harbour master, shipmaster, tugmaster and port controllers will need to be involved and detailed written planning is necessary. The simplest task such as coming to an anchor is worthy of careful thought before being committed to any course of action. After all, to plan any future shiphandling task, one needs to know (a) where one is now, (b) where one will probably be at some given time in the future and (c) the limiting factors on arrival.

The planning of a manoeuvre is directly related to the practice of navigation, and the accuracy of this work is generally proportional to the distance off the nearest danger. For example, a ship on a normal commercial passage will be little worried if her mid-ocean position is accurate to plus or minus five miles whereas such error in the Thames Estuary would be disastrous. In close quarters situations with other vessels or when near to land it is vital that the present relationship is known and that the closer the proximity, up to the point of no return, the greater the accuracy required. The angle of approach to a berth is critical, and if the initial position is not known or appreciated then the angles cannot be measured.

This basic concept of planning a manoeuvre and then having a clear idea of one's intentions is demonstrated in every class of students who undergo training in coxing a ship's lifeboat. Those who consider the wind, tide and propulsive forces before choosing a suitable approach, and also anticipate events by several seconds, will always make a reasonable attempt at the required task. If an error is made they will have time to correct it. If the external forces change, perhaps a gust of wind, then the coxswain, with time and space in hand, will use it to counter the disturbing force.

How then does one start planning a shiphandling exercise? Firstly a sound theoretical knowledge is beneficial in those areas of applied physics and mathematics relevant to a vessel's manoeuvring characteristics. These must include some understanding of the resolution of forces, hydrostatics, hydrodynamics, meteorology, oceanography, tidal theory, wave theory, and theory of levers, marine engineering and navigation. Secondly, an insight into the local conditions is very important. This may be gained by either studying the charts and pilot books or by previous visits. In the majority of ports the employment of a pilot is required and it is of course his duty to advise the shiphandler or master on these conditions. The prudent mariner must not however abdicate his responsibility to the pilot. He cannot in law and should not in practice. It is probable that the chances of a marine pilot making an error are no more and no less than those of any other professional man, which would mean that the odds are quite long but not long enough to be ignored. The person in charge of the bridge should be aware of the planned progress of the ship so that, in the unlikely event of his adviser either giving wrong information or no longer being available, he can bring the ship to a safe mooring.

Armed with the knowledge and experience of what the ship is capable of doing and with up-to-date information on the status of the environment which the vessel is about to enter, detailed plans can now be made. On a large tanker, for example, approaching Western Europe, these plans must include provision for the correct use of *traffic separation schemes* on entering the English Channel and alterations in handling characteristics due to decreasing under keel clearance. Intelligence of conditions ahead, particularly at the port of destination, should be obtained so that speed can be adjusted, if required, to avoid waiting in a congested harbour entrance for the berthing time. Is the port heavily congested, and if so, what are the delays? Do you have adequate charts of the area and is the navigational information up-to-date? Is the navigation and communications equipment operating efficiently? It is unreasonable and perhaps unsafe to expect the commanding officer to remain on the bridge for many hours, as his own efficiency must inevitably decrease with time, therefore are the watchkeeping personnel aware of the ship's intended plan and any constraints upon it?

Organisation

The questions posed above lead us to the next stage of the operation. When a plan of action has been decided, the necessary personnel and resources must be available to ensure a successful conclusion to the operation. This will include such straightforward jobs as clearing away the anchors, making mooring gear ready, ordering tugs, etc. Attention to detail at this stage pays great dividends when the task is underway. Murphy's Law is said to state that 'if there is a possible way of doing something wrong, then someone will find it'. The cynic might suggest that Murphy was employed aboard a ship! It is imperative that the organisation of a manoeuvre or series of manoeuvres is preceded by careful checks as to the muster of equipment, the successful completion of tests of basic controls and information sources such as the steering, engine telegraph, compasses, whistle, tachometers and indicators.

Personnel who are to be involved should be made aware of the requirements of their section and in particular of any critical parts of the operation which will need their special attention. Under certain circumstances the extremities of the ship might screen an object of danger and thus the bridge must rely on information sent from the forecastle or poop. The officer in charge at these stations should have been briefed as to the importance of this data and should be capable of estimating distances reasonably accurately. Industrial safety is of ever increasing importance and the penalties for negligence can no longer be hidden behind small print. The operational organisation must be safe and, where elements of danger do exist, precautions must be taken to warn those involved and to see that they have been adequately trained and that protective clothing, goggles, and safety harnesses are used when necessary. One point often neglected is to keep the engine room crew informed of the plan and the requirements on them, including any details of unusual events which may involve their participation (above all do not forget to ring 'Finished with Engines' when the ship is safely secured).

The best of plans can come unstuck as a result of poor organisation. One of the best ways of ensuring that routine tasks are performed before manoeuvring is to use a check list such as those contained in the International Chamber of Shipping *Bridge Procedure Guide*.

Commanding

Having prepared a plan and organised one's resources, an executive signal, or command, must be given to put the operation into motion. This sounds dramatic but it need not be. The absence of precise instruction is bad practice and should be avoided. For example the mere presence of the ship's captain on the bridge must not inhibit the officer of the watch in his duty, but should a manoeuvre be imminent, requiring the captain to take the con, then a clear instruction should be given to the watchkeeper to this effect, indicating the change of status to all concerned. Nothing can cause more confusion than contrary orders. Should this happen it leads to a lack of confidence and respect by those in subordinate positions.

A positive decision is also important for clearing one's own mind. The sequence of events then follows a systematic progression with the preparatory phases over the active part beginning. The thought processes can then be cleared of planning and organising, for full concentration on the task in hand. It is perhaps inevitable that an often repeated manoeuvre will cause the pulse rate to stay nearer to normal, but it is good practice to firmly take command of the situation. The saying that 'familiarity breeds contempt' is never more true than when leadership is involved. Apparent indecision and lack of real authority heralds a slap-happy approach by those in responsible positions further down the chain of command. In commercial shipping this kind of discipline can be achieved by showing firmness and giving clear instructions (a military manner is neither advisable nor enforceable).

Co-ordinating

Having started with a clear order, the shiphandler's next managerial function is to make sure that all the necessary personnel and equipment in the planned operation are available to play their part when required. By its very nature a ship is a self-contained and self-sufficient unit requiring little outside support for its journeyings. There are, however, certain items which do require co-ordination such as the presence of tugs or mooring gangs. These would have been ordered during the preparation phase but it is now important to check that they are waiting in the appointed place before being committed to a part of the operation which may not be easy to reverse. Similarly, on a long voyage it is likely that bunkering and stores will be required en-route. A radio message must be sent off to the agents in the proposed port of call to arrange for such fuel and provisions.

On-board co-ordination is vital to the success of the voyage. Fortunately, in most ships, standards of seamanship and professional discipline are high and the need for the ship's captain to exercise his authority is minimal, but that authority must remain in reserve and should be used if the operational functions of the ship, her officers and crew, start to slide. It is a noticeable feature of many collision and grounding reports that the basic cause of the mishap is a failure to right a malpractice or correct an error which itself is not critical, but when taken in conjunction with another unrelated event can lead to a serious incident. The co-ordination of navigational procedures may be slack, such as the omission of a regular position on the chart. Such a practice may not alone make a stranding inevitable, but when coupled with an event such as a total electrical failure, the results of the negligence may well lead to catastrophy.

This phase of the operation is obviously improved as teamwork aboard the ship is developed, which is of course the principal objective of the computerised ship's bridge simulators now being used for training programmes by many of the leading maritime nations.

Controlling

With the operation underway and the systems employed apparently working, it is now necessary to enter the fifth and perhaps most important phase. That of measuring the effectiveness of the operation. The task may be a simple one such as weighing anchor but how does the master know that the order to 'heave away' was received and is being obeyed? Obviously a communications system must exist between the bridge and forecastle head. On a small vessel this is done by simply leaning over the bridge front and using direct communications by voice and hand signal. The responses come back from the bells being made to indicate the shackles coming over the gypsy, the groans of the windlass and the officer in charge indicating with his arm the direction in which the cable is 'growing'.

On larger ships the communications are by telephone, a talk back system or very often these days by hand-held radio telephones as the short-range methods will not work. It is imperative that messages by any of these means are clear and that the person in charge receives accurate information. It is the sole justification for technical language, that those in the profession are trained to understand the precise meaning of technical terminology which may be nonsense to the layman. This is not to be confused with slang or fashionable language. These comments apply particularly to radio telephone procedures where messages must not only be transmitted accurately but the identity of the station must be clear. A story is told of a well known shipping company issuing 'walkie-talkie' sets to its ships which were all tuned to the same frequency. When the master of one ship, approaching the anchorage off Singapore, ordered 'Let go!' chains were heard to rattle out of the hawse pipes of half the ships in harbour.

It is by these various means that information is conveyed to and from the commander to tell him of the progress of the ship during the manoeuvre which he has initiated, and which now enables him to issue supplementary instructions.

Communications can take many forms. Instructions are given to the engine room by a telegraph or by direct control. The effect of these orders is confirmed by watching a tachometer, the log and by visual observation after its receipt is first acknowledged. Further messages may come from rate of turn indicators, compass repeaters and navigational instruments. The purpose of this information is for the shiphandler to ascertain whether or not the operation is proceeding according to the plan.

The quality of navigational data is of particular importance because it is a measure of the ship's progress along the planned course. The principal reason for the officer of the watch regularly marking the chart with the ship's position is to plot the *track* of the vessel so that it can be related to the intended path. If there is a discrepancy then corrective action should be taken. This action will usually be a small angular adjustment to the ship's heading to bring about a return to the planned course line. In an emergency situation it may be necessary to stop the ship and perhaps reverse the course being steered.

Navigational control is of two main types. The first of these is *dead reckoning* where a deduction of the ship's position is made, based on the direction and distance moved since the last known observed position. This DR might be modified by adding components thought to be appropriate for the prevailing effects of wind and tide, in which case the position plotted is referred to as an *estimated position*. At their simplest, DR positions are obtained from the compass course and distance run by log. However, far greater accuracy can be obtained by using an inertial navigation system which works by measuring the ship's movement through its effect on very sensitive instrumentation. With either type of measuring device the error will increase with time.

This error must be detected, which is done by the second and more important method of navigational control, the *observed* or *fixed position*. This 'fix' relates the ship's position to that of known objects. The method employed may be visual, by observing terrestrial or celestial objects, aural by listening to and timing reflected sounds, or by the observation of some aspect of radio propagation which is measured and then, by use of principles of physics, related to known patterns. Alternatively, simple physical measurement can be employed by using a sounding line to determine the depth of water. Although a sounding may not pinpoint the ship's position, it will frequently show where the vessel is not (which can be very reassuring).

As indicated above, the accuracy required will vary with the risk and the operation. The degree of control therefore varies accordingly. On passage in mid-ocean, positional checks are made perhaps three times a day by astronomical means. If Omega, Loran or satellite systems are available, then a greater frequency of observation is possible and desirable. Furthermore each should be used to check the other because it is not unknown for errors to occur in electronic navigational aids whereas astro-fixes do not require any information external to the ship except an occasional time check for the chronometer, nor do they need any electrical power from the ship's supply.

As the ship approaches coastal waters, the navigational control will increase and, due to the traffic becoming denser, collision avoidance control will also be stepped up. On the navigational side, there are two obvious areas where the accuracy improves, namely the scale of chart in use and the time interval between fixes. Visual sightings of terrestrial objects may be possible and should be used as a cross-check on electronic aids like the Decca Navigator and radar. The interval between fixes is now reduced to perhaps every fifteen minutes and should the ship be found to be off the planned course or have to deviate because of her obligations under the collision regulations, action will be taken to resume the passage along the intended path. Thus control is continually being exercised to measure and correct variations from the course line and if there is flexibility in the speed it may also be adjusted to make a chosen estimated time of arrival. The watch status has probably increased to having steering in manual control and a second person on the bridge to assist the officer of the watch. The ship's captain will also visit the bridge more frequently to monitor progress and as the shiphandling problems increase, in poor visibility and in heavy traffic, he will take over the watch.

As the ship nears her port of destination, the degree of control will be increased to enable navigational accuracy to be improved further, and reaction to the collision regulations to be immediate when required. The engines will be ready for changes of direction or revolutions and the forecastle manned so that anchors can be let go quickly should the need arise. A pilot, whose job it is to advise the ship's captain on local matters, will probably be employed for these latter stages of the voyage. Perhaps, if the circumstances warrant, responsibility may be delegated to the pilot by the captain for him to take operational charge of the bridge. If this is the case the captain and the officer of the watch must continue to measure progress by plotting the ship's position and must be aware of the planned events which are anticipated to occur in the near future.

Measurement and control of the ship's position and her on-board functions at the terminal points of the voyage are extremely important, because the relationship between the ship, the external forces acting upon the hull and the forces generated by the ship herself, are often at their maximum in restricted waters. When nearing the berth, the angle of approach is critical to the successful docking of the vessel. The speed of approach is also of major importance particularly over the last few metres. The position of the ship, the direction of her movement (which is not necessarily the same as the direction of the ship's head) and her speed, both over the ground and through the water, must be known and appreciated. In smaller vessels this can often be done by eye but as ship size increases in relation to the depth and width of the channel, and as the mass of the vessel becomes greater, the loads on impact with the berth become so critical that physical measurement of the relevant parameters is vital to the successful completion of the voyage.

The concluding part in the control of the task is to log the data obtained. The legal significance of a record of the voyage is well known but equally important, from the point of view of the management of a ship, is the abstract of information on voyage performance. From this information the planning of the next operation or passage can begin. Areas of inefficiency can be identified and those functions within the influence of the ship's personnel can be examined to see if improvements can be effected. No matter what type of vessel one is sailing in, there are lessons to be learned from past voyages to enable future voyage plans, shipboard systems and ship designs to be improved.

Department of Trade Notices

MERCHANT SHIPPING NOTICE NO. M.725

WAVE QUELLING OILS—USE OF OIL IN RESCUE OPERATIONS

(This Notice supersedes Notice No. M.412)

1. The Department of Trade advises seafarers against the indiscriminate use of oil to calm the sea by ships coming to the rescue of other ships. When survivors are likely to be in the water, the pumping of oil should only be carried out when absolutely necessary and then with the greatest care.

2. Experience has shown that vegetable and animal oils, including fish oils, are most suitable in such circumstances. If they are not available, lubricating oils should be used. Fuel oil should not be used unless absolutely unavoidable and then only in very limited quantities. Oils of the former types are less harmful to men in the water and are very effective quelling agents. Tests carried out by an independent company have shown that 200 litres of lubricating oil discharged slowly through a rubber hose with an outlet just above the sea while the ship proceeds at slow speed can be an effective agent for quelling seas over an area of at least 4500 square metres.

MERCHANT SHIPPING NOTICE NO. M.748

SAFETY OF TUGS WHILE TOWING

(This Notice supersedes Notice No. M.466)

Following another casualty to a tug the Department wishes to again emphasise the danger of capsizing which may occur when the tow rope reaches a large angle to the centre line of the tug and the tug is unable to slip her tow.

The tug referred to above was engaged on harbour duties acting as a stern tug and had just commenced to cant a cargo ship, prior to berthing. During the manoeuvre the tow rope reached a position at right angles to the centre line of the tug (a position commonly referred to as 'girting') causing an upsetting moment on the tug to the extent that she capsized and sank, fortunately without loss of life. The casualty became inevitable when the quick release mechanism on the towing hook failed to operate causing her to heel over to such an angle that the sills of the openings were immersed, allowing rapid flooding to occur.

Contributory causes to the casualty were:

  (i) small freeboard
 (ii) poor curve or righting levers
(iii) closing appliances to spaces leading below not secured.

In order to reduce the grave dangers associated with such conditions, particularly with smaller tugs engaged on harbour duties, the Department make the following recommendations:

1. It is of the greatest importance that the design of the towing gear should be such as to minimise the overturning moment due to the lead of the towline and that the towing hook should have a positive means of quick release which can be relied upon to function correctly under ALL operating conditions. It is desirable that the release mechanism should be controlled from the wheelhouse, the after control position (if fitted) and at the hook itself. The local control at the hook should preferably be of the direct mechanical type capable of independent operation. It is also essential that the greatest care should be taken in the maintenance of the towing gear to ensure its full efficiency at all times.

2. Openings in superstructures, deckhouses and exposed machinery casings situated on the weather deck, which provide access to spaces below that deck, should be fitted with weathertight doors which comply with the requirements for weathertight doors contained in paragraph 1 Schedule 4 of the Merchant Shipping (Load Line) Rules 1968. Such doors should be kept closed during towing operations.

Engine room ventilation should be arranged by means of high coaming ventilators and air pipes should be fitted with automatic means of closure.

3. Stability criteria for tugs not subject to the requirements of the Merchant Shipping (Load Line) Rules 1968:

  (i) In the normal working condition, the freeboard should be such that the deck-edge is not immersed at an angle of less than 10°.
 (ii) The GM (feet) in the worst anticipated service condition should not be less than

$$\frac{K}{4f \times C_B}$$

$$\text{where } K = \left[\left(5 + \frac{8L}{100}\right) - 0.45r\right]$$

L = Length of the vessel between perpendiculars (feet)
r = length of radial arm of towing hook (feet)
f = Freeboard (feet)
C_B = block coefficient

Any existing tug which cannot attain the GM calculated in accordance with sub-paragraph (ii) above might nevertheless gain some improvement in her stability by having structures on the weather deck properly closed in accordance with paragraph 2 above.

4. In cases where compliance with the recommendations in paragraphs 2 and 3 cannot readily be attained consideration should be given to:

(*a*) substitution of permanent ballast for water ballast and conversion of peak ballast spaces to dry spaces

(*b*) fitting a permanent device to minimise the possibility of the tow lead coming into the athwartship position.

5. In the case of tugs which proceed to sea and are subject to the requirements of the Merchant Shipping (Load Line) Rules 1968 the stability criteria to be achieved and approved by the Department are as laid down in Schedule 4 Part I para 2 of those rules.

MERCHANT SHIPPING NOTICE NO. 753

PILOT LADDERS AND MECHANICAL PILOT HOISTS

(This Notice supersedes Notices Nos. 640 and 644)

1. Attention is drawn to IMCO Resolution A.275(VIII)—Recommendation on Performance Standards for Mechanical Pilot Hoists—which sets out performance criteria for the design, construction, testing and operation of pilot hoists. These recommended standards are reproduced in the Annex to this Notice.

2. Apart from hoists already fitted, or supplied for vessels under construction, the Department will only recommend acceptance of the design of pilot hoists which meet these standards in every respect. Manufacturers of pilot hoists are advised to submit to the Department designs that are in strict accordance with the relevant provisions.

3. Where a pilot hoist is provided, personnel engaged in rigging and operating it should be fully instructed in the safe procedures to be adopted and the equipment should be tested prior to the embarkation or disembarkation of a pilot. Provision of a pilot hoist does not relieve owners and masters of the statutory duty to provide a pilot ladder which complies with the requirements of Rule 4 of the Merchant Shipping (Pilot Ladders) Rules 1965 as amended by the Merchant Shipping (Pilot Ladders) (Amendment No. 2) Rules 1972. The ladder should be available adjacent to the hoist in case there is a failure of the source of power or the pilot prefers to use the pilot ladder.

4. Furthermore, the Department wishes to stress the need for strict compliance with the Rules in order to minimise the danger to pilots when boarding and leaving ships. Particular attention should be given to the following points:

(a) Pilot ladders should be rigged so that they are not too high from the water and in such a manner that the steps are horizontal.

(b) Pilot ladders constructed with large triangular wooden inserts above and below the steps cause difficulty in grasping the side ropes and their use is not recommended.

(c) When an accommodation ladder is used in conjunction with a pilot ladder, the pilot ladder should be positioned in such a manner as to afford easy and safe access to the accommodation ladder platform.

(d) The rigging of pilot ladders and the embarkation and disembarkation of pilots must be supervised by a responsible officer of the ship.

MERCHANT SHIPPING NOTICE NO. M.792

INTERACTION BETWEEN SHIPS

1. A number of casualties to ships have been caused or contributed to by the phenomenon of hydrodynamic interaction between ships in near proximity to each other. They have fallen into two categories: cases where ships were attempting to pass one another at very close range, due usually to their being confined to a narrow channel, and cases where ships have been necessarily manoeuvring in very close company for operational reasons. Particularly in the first type of case there have often been additional complications in the presence of bank suction or rejection, and of shallow water effect. (An appendix to this notice summarises the conclusion of recent laboratory work on this subject.)

2. So far as passing at close range is concerned, interaction is most

likely to prove dangerous in overtaking cases, where there are two possibilities: the ship being overtaken may take a sheer into the path of the other; or the two ships may repel each other when they are abeam, causing the bows to turn away and the sterns to swing together. With a head-on encounter interaction is less likely to have a dangerous effect as generally the bows of the two ships will tend to repel each other as they approach. However, this can lead indirectly to a critical situation: in many cases the vessel will already be altering to starboard (assuming that a normal port-to-port passing is intended), when the effect is to increase the swing, probably causing port helm to be applied to check it: if the ship has now approached the edge of the channel and feels bank rejection a marked and possibly perilous port sheer will develop.

3. When therefore ships intend to pass in a narrow channel, whether on the same or opposing courses (*a*) each ship should endeavour so far as possible to pass mid-way between the other and the edge of the channel; (*b*) any alteration of course needed to do this should be made in good time before the effects of interaction are felt; (*c*) the helm should be used quickly to counter any sheer and then smartly brought amidships ready to meet any reverse swing; (*d*) speed should be sufficient for it to be reduced without causing loss of steerage way, but below the maximum so that in an emergency some extra power is in hand to aid the rudder.

4. The other type of case, where ships are manoeuvring at close quarters for operational reasons, has most potential danger when one of the ships is a good deal larger than the other, and this most commonly occurs in normal merchant service operations when a ship is being attended by a tug. A dangerous situation is most likely when the tug, having been steaming alongside the ship, moves ahead to the bow as when preparing to pass or take a tow-line. Due to changes in drag effects, especially in shallow water, the tug has at first to exert appreciably more ahead power than the larger ship and this effect is strongest when she is off the shoulder. At that point also hydrodynamic forces tend to deflect the tug's bow away from the ship and attract her stern; but as she draws ahead the reverse occurs, the stern being strongly repulsed, and the increased drag largely disappears. There is thus a strong tendency to develop a sheer towards the ship, and unless the helm, which will have been put towards the ship to counter the previous effect, is very smartly reversed and engine revolutions very quickly reduced the tug may well drive herself under the ship's bow. Further, another effect of interaction arises from the flow around the larger ship acting on the underbody of the smaller vessel causing a consequent decrease in effective stability, and thus increasing the likelihood of capsize if the ships touch. Since it has been found that the strength of hydrodynamic interaction varies approximately as the square of the speed, this sort of manoeuvre should

always be carried out at very slow speed indeed. If ships of disparate size are to work in close company at any higher speed then it is essential that the smaller vessel keeps clear of the hazardous area off the other's bow.

5. A recent casualty exemplifies the dangers. A cargo ship of some 1600 tons gross, in ballast, was approaching a British port and was to be assisted to her berth by a harbour tug. The mean draughts of the ship and the tug were respectively 9′ 0″ and 7′ 0″. The tug was instructed to make fast on the starboard bow as the ship was proceeding inwards, and to do this she first paralleled her course and then gradually drew ahead so that her towing deck was abeam of the ship's forecastle, distant some 15–20 feet. The speed of the two ships was about 4 knots through the water, the ship steaming at slow ahead and the tug, in order to counteract drag, at ¾ speed. As the tow line was being passed the tug took a sheer to port and before this could be countered the two vessels touched, the ship's stem striking the tug's port quarter. The impact was no more than a bump but even so the tug took an immediate starboard list, and within a few seconds capsized. One man was drowned.

APPENDIX

Extensive laboratory work was recently carried out on the combined effect of hydrodynamic interaction and shallow water (i.e. depth of water less than about twice the draught) and the following conclusions, which accord with practical experience, were among those reached:

(*a*) The effects of interaction (and also of bank suction and rejection) are amplified in shallow water.

(*b*) The effectiveness of the rudder is reduced in shallow water, and depends very much on adequate propeller speed. The minimum revolutions needed to maintain steerage way may therefore be higher than are required in deep water.

(*c*) However, relatively high speeds in very shallow water must be avoided due to the danger of grounding because of squat. An increase in draught of well over 10% has been observed at speeds of about 10 knots, but when speed is reduced squat rapidly diminishes.

(*d*) The transverse thrust of the propeller changes in strength and may even act in the reverse sense to normal.

(*e*) Ships may therefore experience quite marked changes in their manoeuvring characteristics as the depth of water under the keel changes. In particular, when the under keel clearance is very small a marked loss of turning ability is likely.

Further information is available from the National Maritime Institute,

Faggs Road, Feltham, Middlesex, who have recently completed a film entitled 'Interaction' in co-operation with the Nautical Institute.

MERCHANT SHIPPING NOTICE NO. M.795

TOWS

(This Notice supersedes M.733)

1. Following several incidents in the North Sea, a Notice was issued in November 1975, to remind all involved in navigation and offshore operations in that area of the particular dangers posed by vessels under tow. Since that time there have been further incidents including collisions with unlit tows and hawsers or attachments parting due to inadequate strength or because they have been snagged on the seabed.

2. As a result of the continuing occurrence of such incidents and the associated hazards to navigation, the Department, in consultation with the industry, has now produced recommendations for those engaged in towage operations. (These recommendations are set out in the Appendix to this Notice.)

3. If a uniformly high standard of towage practice is to be achieved, it is essential that the recommendations are observed by all concerned. Although the incidents have so far been mainly confined to the North Sea, the recommendations are generally applicable to all towage operations.

4. The 1972 Collision Regulations come into force on 15 July 1977, from which date a vessel towing will be required to show a yellow towing light, in addition to the previously required lights, and to show extra lights or shapes if a towing operation renders her unable to deviate from her course. Furthermore, a towing vessel can attract attention by directing the beam of a searchlight in the direction of the tow (Rules 24, 27, 36 and Annex 1 of the 1972 Collision Regulations refer).

5. All those involved in towage operations and in navigating are reminded of the obligation to keep a proper look-out under the Collision Regulations (Rule 5 of the 1972 Collision Regulations) and their attention is drawn once more to the recommendations concerning the keeping of a safe navigational watch as contained in IMCO Resolution A285 (VIII) and in M Notice 756.

6. When a manned tow is planned, the Department of Trade must be consulted in good time. It will be necessary to comply with all statutory safety requirements including those for life-saving appliances, fire appliances and radio. Whether manned or not any vessel towed to sea must

be issued with a load line certificate or a load line exemption· certificate. A list of Principal Regulations on Merchant Shipping is set out in M Notice 785.

APPENDIX

Recommendations

1. The route to be followed by the tow is to be planned in advance taking into account such factors as the weather, tidal streams and currents, the size, shape and weight of the tow and the navigational hazards to be avoided. Careful consideration is to be given to the number of towing vessels to be employed.

2. There is to be contingency planning to cover the onset of bad weather particularly in respect of arrangements for heaving to or taking shelter.

3. The towing arrangements are to be suitable for the particular tow and the towing gear is to be adequate and of suitable strength.

4. The towing operation is to be in the charge of a competent tow master. Other towing personnel are to be suitably experienced and sufficient in number.

5.1 Wherever practicable, secondary or emergency towing arrangements are to be fitted on board the tow so as to be easily recoverable by the towing vessel in the event of a breakage of the prime towing wire or ancillary equipment.

5.2 In all cases, the arrangements for recovering the tow, should it break adrift, are to be made in accordance with good seamanship practice having in mind the seasonal weather conditions and area of operation.

6.1 All those responsible for tows are reminded of their obligation to see that the tows are lit in accordance with the International Regulations for Preventing Collisions at Sea and similarly that the towing vessels also exhibit the correct lights.

6.2 Due consideration must be given to the fitting of lighting systems, the reliability of the lights and their ability to function for long periods unattended in all foreseeable conditions. It is most desirable that a duplicate system of lights be provided.

7. Prior to sailing, the watertight integrity of the tow should be assured by an inspection of the closing arrangements for all hatches, valves, airpipes, and any other openings through which water might enter the hull. The tow should be at a suitable draught for the intended passage. Where the tow is manned, there should be appropriate arrangements for ballasting it to a condition in which it will survive bad weather.

8. The securing arrangements for the cargo and stores carried on the

tow are to be carefully examined to ensure that they are adequate for the duration of the voyage, especially on an unmanned tow. The stowage of deck cargo should be so arranged as to provide the tow with adequate stability.

9. Lifesaving appliances in the form of lifejackets and lifebuoys must be provided whenever personnel are on board the tow even if only for short periods.

10. HM Coastguard are to be informed in advance of the intended passage of a difficult tow; after sailing the Coastguard or Coast Radio Station should be kept informed of the movement. Where tows through breaking adrift or other cause present a potential hazard to shipping or offshore structures, the accompanying towing vessel should immediately take steps to broadcast an Urgency Signal.

11. Before departure, the towing vessel and tow, and the towage and stowage arrangements are to be inspected by the tow master and another competent person who are to agree that everything is satisfactory.

MERCHANT SHIPPING NOTICE NO. M.854

NAVIGATION SAFETY

1. Research into recent accidents occurring to ships has shown that by far the most important contributory cause of navigational accidents is human error, and in many cases information which could have prevented the accident was available to those responsible for the navigation of the ships concerned.

2. There is no evidence to show serious deficiency on the part of deck officers with respect either to basic training in navigation skills or ability to use navigational instruments and equipment; but accidents happen because one person makes the sort of mistake to which all human beings are prone in a situation where there is no navigational regime constantly in use which might enable the mistake to be detected before an accident occurs.

3. To assist masters and deck officers to appreciate the risks to which they are exposed and to provide help in reducing these risks it is recommended that steps are taken to:

(*a*) ensure that all the ship's navigation is planned in adequate detail with contingency plans where appropriate;

(*b*) ensure that there is a systematic bridge organisation that provides for:

(i) comprehensive briefing of all concerned with the navigation of the ship;

(ii) close and continuous monitoring of the ship's position ensuring as far as possible that different means of determining position are used to check against error in any one system;

(iii) cross-checking of individual human decisions so that errors can be detected and corrected as early as possible;

(iv) information available from plots of other traffic to be used carefully to ensure against over-confidence, bearing in mind that other ships may alter course and speed.

(c) ensure that optimum and systematic use is made of all information that becomes available to the navigational staff;

(d) ensure that all the intentions of a pilot are fully understood and acceptable to the ship's navigational staff.

4. The Annex to this Notice provides information on the planning and conduct of passages which may prove useful to mariners.

(ANNEX)

GUIDE TO THE PLANNING AND CONDUCT OF PASSAGES

Pilotage

1. The contribution which pilots make to the safety of navigation in confined waters and port approaches, of which they have up-to-date knowledge, requires no emphasis; but it should be stressed that the responsibilities of the ship's navigational team do not transfer to the pilot and the duties of the officer of the watch remain with that officer.

2. After his arrival on board, in addition to being advised by the master of the manoeuvring characteristics and basic details of the vessel for its present condition of loading, the pilot should be clearly consulted on the passage plan to be followed. The general aim of the master should be to ensure that the expertise of the pilot is fully supported by the ship's bridge team. (See also paragraph 16.)

3. Attention is drawn to the following extract from IMCO Resolution A 285 (VIII):

"Despite the duties and obligations of a pilot, his presence on board does not relieve the officer of the watch from his duties and obligations for the safety of the ship. He should co-operate closely with the pilot and maintain an accurate check on the vessel's position and movements. If he is in any doubt as to the pilot's actions or intentions, he should seek clarification from the pilot and if doubt still exists he should notify the master immediately and take whatever action is necessary before the master arrives."

Responsibility for Passage Planning

4. In most deep-sea ships it is customary for the master to delegate the initial responsibility for preparing the plan for a passage to the officer responsible for navigational equipment and publications, usually the second officer. For the purposes of this guide the officer concerned will be referred to as the navigating officer.

5. It will be evident that in small ships, including fishing vessels, the master or skipper may himself need to exercise the responsibility of the navigating officer for passage planning purposes.

6. The navigating officer has the task of preparing the detailed passage plan to the master's requirements prior to departure. In those cases when the port of destination is not known or is subsequently altered, it will be necessary for the navigating officer to extend or amend the original plan as appropriate.

Principles of Passage Planning

7. There are four distinct stages in the planning and achievement of a safe passage:

1. Appraisal
2. Planning
3. Execution
4. Monitoring

8. These stages must of necessity follow each other in the order set out above. An appraisal of information available must be made before detailed plans can be drawn up and a plan must be in existence before tactics for its execution can be decided upon. Once the plan and the manner in which it is to be executed have been decided, monitoring must be carried out to ensure that the plan is followed.

Appraisal

9. This is the process of gathering together all information relevant to the contemplated passage. It will of course be concerned with navigational information shown on charts and in publications such as sailing directions, light lists, current atlas, tidal atlas, tide tables, Notices to Mariners, publications detailing traffic separation and other routeing schemes, and radio aids to navigation. Reference should also be made to climatic data and other appropriate meteorological information which may have a bearing upon the availability for use of navigational aids in

the area under consideration such as, for example, those areas subject to periods of reduced visibility.

10. A check list should be available for the use of the navigating officer to assist him to gather all the information necessary for a full passage appraisal and the circumstances under which it is to be made. It is necessary to recognise that more up-to-date information, for example, radio navigational warnings and meteorological forecasts, may be received after the initial appraisal.

11. In addition to the obvious requirement for charts to cover the area or areas through which the ship will proceed, which should be checked to see that they are corrected up to date in respect of both permanent and temporary Notices to Mariners and existing radio navigational warnings, the information necessary to make an appraisal of the intended passage will include details of:

(*a*) Currents (direction and rate of set)
(*b*) Tides (times, heights and direction of rate of set)
(*c*) Draught of ship during the various stages of the intended passage
(*d*) Advice and recommendations given in sailing directions
(*e*) Navigational lights (characteristics, range, arc of visibility and anticipated raising range)
(*f*) Navigational marks (anticipating range at which objects will show on radar and/or will be visible to the eye)
(*g*) Traffic separation and routeing schemes
(*h*) Radio aids to navigation (availability and coverage of Decca, Omega, Loran and D/F and degree of accuracy of each in that locality)
(*i*) Navigational warnings affecting the area
(*j*) Climatological data affecting the area
(*k*) Ship's manoeuvring data.

12. An overall assessment of the intended passage should be made by the master, in consultation with the navigating officer and other deck officers who will be involved, when all relevant information has been gathered. This appraisal will provide the master and his bridge team with a clear and precise indication of all areas of danger, and delineate the areas in which it will be possible to navigate safely taking into account the calculated draught of the ship and planned under-keel clearance. Bearing in mind the condition of the ship, her equipment and any other circumstances, a balanced judgement of the margins of safety which must be allowed in the various sections of the intended passage can now be made, agreed and understood by all concerned.

Planning

13. Having made the fullest possible appraisal using all the available information on board relating to the intended passage, the navigating officer can now act upon the master's instructions to prepare a detailed plan of the passage. The detailed plan should embrace the whole passage, from berth to berth, and include all waters where a pilot will be on board.

14. The formulation of the plan will involve completion of the following tasks:

(a) Plot the intended passage on the appropriate charts and mark clearly, on the largest scale charts applicable, all areas of danger and the intended track taking into account the margins of allowable error. Where appropriate, due regard should be paid to the need for advance warning to be given on one chart of the existence of a navigational hazard immediately on transfer to the next. The planned track should be plotted to clear hazards at as safe a distance as circumstances allow. A longer distance should always be accepted in preference to a shorter more hazardous route. The possibility of main engine or steering gear breakdown at a critical moment must not be overlooked.

(b) Indicate clearly in 360 degree notation the true direction of the planned track marked on the charts.

(c) Mark on the chart those radar conspicuous objects, ramarks or racons, which may be used in position fixing.

(d) Mark on the charts any transit marks, clearing bearings or clearing ranges (radar) which may be used to advantage. It is sometimes possible to use two conspicuous clearing marks where a line drawn through them runs clear of natural dangers with the appropriate margin of safety; if the ship proceeds on the safe side of this transit she will be clear of the danger. If no clearing marks are available, a line or lines of bearings from a single object may be drawn at a desired safe distance from the danger; provided the ship remains in the safe segment, she will be clear of the danger.

(e) Decide upon the key elements of the navigational plan. These should include but not be limited to:

(i) safe speed having regard to the manoeuvring characteristics of the ship and, in ships restricted by draught, due allowance for reduction of draught due to squat and heel effect when turning;

(ii) speed alterations necessary to achieve desired ETA's en route, e.g. where there may be limitations on night passage, tidal restrictions etc.;

(iii) positions where a change in machinery status is required;
(iv) course alteration points, with wheel-over positions; where appropriate on large scale charts taking into account the ship's turning circle at the planned speed and the effect of any tidal stream or current on the ship's movement during the turn;
(v) minimum clearance required under the keel in critical areas (having allowed for height of tide);
(vi) points where accuracy of position fixing is critical, and the primary and secondary methods by which such positions must be obtained for maximum reliability;
(vii) contingency plans for alternative action to place the ship in deep water or proceed to an anchorage in the event of any emergency necessitating abandonment of the plan.

15. Depending on circumstances, the main details of the plan referred to in paragraph 14 above should be marked in appropriate and prominent places on the charts to be used during the passage. These main details of the passage plan should in any case be recorded in a bridge notebook used specially for this purpose to allow reference to details of the plan at the conning position without the need to consult the chart. Supporting information relative to the passage such as times of high and low water, or of sunrise or sunset, should also be recorded in this notebook.

16. It is unlikely that every detail of a passage will have been anticipated, particularly in pilotage waters. Much of what will have been planned may have to be changed after embarking the pilot. This in no way detracts from the real value of the plan, which is to mark out in advance where the ship must *not* go and the precautions which must be taken to achieve that end, or to give initial warning that the ship is standing into danger.

Execution

17. Having finalised the passage plan, and as soon as estimated times of arrival can be made with reasonable accuracy, the tactics to be used in the execution of the plan should be decided. The factors to be taken into account will include:

(*a*) the reliability and condition of the ship's navigational equipment;
(*b*) estimated times of arrival at critical points for tide heights and flow;
(*c*) meteorological conditions, particularly in areas known to be affected by frequent periods of low visibility;
(*d*) daytime versus night-time passing of danger points, and any effect this may have upon position fixing accuracy;

(*e*) traffic conditions, especially at navigational focal points.

18. It will be important for the master to consider whether any particular circumstance, such as the forecast of restricted visibility in an area where position fixing by visual means at a critical point is an essential feature of the navigation plan, introduces an unacceptable hazard to the safe conduct of the passage; and thus whether that section of the passage should be attempted under the conditions prevailing, or likely to prevail. He should also consider at which specific points of the passage he may need to utilise additional deck or engine room personnel.

Monitoring

19. The close and continuous monitoring of the ship's progress along the pre-planned track is essential for the safe conduct of the passage. If the officer of the watch is ever in any doubt as to the position of the ship or the manner in which the passage is proceeding he should immediately call the master and, if necessary, take whatever action he may think necessary for the safety of the ship.

20. The performance of navigational equipment should be checked prior to sailing, prior to entering restricted or hazardous waters and at regular and frequent intervals at other times throughout the passage.

21. Advantage should be taken of all the navigational equipment with which the ship is fitted for position monitoring, bearing in mind the following points:

(*a*) visual bearings are usually the most accurate means of position fixing;

(*b*) every fix should, if possible, be based on at least three position lines;

(*c*) transit marks, clearing bearings and clearing ranges (radar) can be of great assistance;

(*d*) when checking, use systems which are based on different data;

(*e*) positions obtained by navigational aids should be checked where practicable by visual means;

(*f*) the value of the echo sounder as a navigational aid;

(*g*) buoys should not be used for fixing but may be used for guidance when shore marks are difficult to distinguish visually; in these circumstances their positions should first be checked by other means;

(*h*) the functioning and correct reading of the instruments used should be checked;

(*i*) an informed decision in advance as to the frequency with which the position is to be fixed should be made for each section of the passage.

22. On every occasion when the ship's position is fixed and marked on the chart in use, the estimated position at a convenient interval of time in advance should be projected and plotted.

23. Radar can be used to advantage in monitoring the position of the ship by the use of parallel indexing techniques. Parallel indexing, as a simple and most effective way of continuously monitoring a ship's progress in restricted waters, can be used in any situation where a radar-conspicuous navigation mark is available and it is practicable to monitor continuously the ship's position relative to such an object.

Department of Trade
Marine Division

Author's Note. The above notices have been included because they are relevant to the text. They were in force at the time of writing but may well be superseded by newer material. The reader is therefore advised to consult an up-to-date file of 'M' notices to seek the latest advice of the Department of Trade.

Index